AF413597

If I Had To Do It Again...

An Internet Entrepreneur's Wisdom in Hindsight

IF I HAD TO DO IT AGAIN

INTERNET ENTREPRENEURS' WISDOM IN HINDSIGHT

SANJAY MEHTA &
HAREESH TIBREWALA

notionpress.com

INDIA · SINGAPORE · MALAYSIA

An Introduction

This is the story of two friends – Sanjay Mehta and Hareesh Tibrewala – whose undying passion for new-age business saw them tread through a very interesting entrepreneurial journey. *If I Had To Do It Again* is a memoir of their experiences, their learning and the wisdom they had accumulated in the process, which they believe every budding entrepreneur can use.

Their venture may not have turned out exactly the way as was expected, but with grit, determination and patience, they were able to sail through. What steps to take when a venture fails to turn out the way as expected? What decisions to make when the business is hitting a new low? These are situations that budding entrepreneurs may be able to relate to. This book highlights what to do under such circumstances and how to make the best of the situation.

The new generation entrepreneurs can use the 'ups' mentioned in the book as an inspiration, and the 'downs' as a reference to avoid similar situations for themselves. Dedicated to all those enthusiastic entrepreneurs who are dreaming of building a business empire, Sanjay and Hareesh feel their story can play a small, yet meaningful role, in fulfilling their dreams.

Our Story

We co-founded an Internet start up way back in 1998. Those were very early days for the Internet and Internet businesses in India. Those were exciting, yet very challenging times.

There is always a lot of passion and fun in starting one's own venture. And if that happens to be in a new-age business, the excitement is double. Yet, being a pioneer in the space, there are no precedents to learn from, no idols to worship, no tracks to follow. It is like walking through a dark alley, feeling your way around, advancing bit by bit, changing tracks a little when needed and trying to ensure that you were somehow moving ahead. We also found ourselves in such a situation and it was challenging indeed!

Then followed the dot com boom in 1999-2000, when the Internet industry became the cynosure of all eyes, when everyone wanted to reach out to us, when we had our 15 seconds of fame, when investors wanted to pump money into our venture, when employees were willing to leave cosy jobs to come and work with us.

Oh, those heady days…

But as they say - what goes up, comes down. And what goes up very fast might also come crashing down as quickly. That was what the dotcom bust in 2000-2001 did to us. We came crashing down. The Internet and dotcom became curse words, investors jumped off leaving the ships to fend for themselves, employees who could return to their earlier jobs retreated quickly, and advertisers disappeared.

Oh, those down-in-the-dump days…

Unlike many others who decided to wind up their Internet ventures, we saw in ours a genuine business model. We decided to stick around and run the company. In the process, we went through an extremely tough phase between 2001-2004. We survived on meager money, moved to a smaller office that did not even have air-conditioners, figured out a way to grow a consumer focused business without any serious marketing budgets - we did it all. And we managed to bring our business to the black for the very first time.

2005-2006 was the period of consolidation, of attempting new growth strategies, of expecting to get value for having survived the toughest period and trying to raise money to take the business to the next level. Not realising that the game had changed. That the carpet had moved from below our feet and we were caught on the wrong foot.

After eight years of struggle, it was time to face the reality - that the big game was not happening. Any serious shift to make our business model work would convert it into a different business altogether. That did not seem to make sense. The only way out was an exit, which we were able to find after some effort. We sold our business to another company in the same space, who were able to consolidate and make 2 and 2 add up to 6.

It was an honourable exit. A dignified one too. But not quite as rewarding as we would have liked it to be. If the monetary benefit was low, the experience and the insight that we had gained over these years were invaluable.

That's our story. At every step, there were lessons to learn. And especially now, looking at it from a distance, we can see many pearls of wisdom in our journey.

*(*By the time, this book goes to print, we will have embarked on our next journey, with Social Wavelength, now rebranded as Mirum, and a part of global digital agency brand of J. Walter Thompson Company. We can say that the lessons were well learnt and the learning was put to good use. But more about it, perhaps in another book, in a few years' time !)*

If I Had To Do It Again...
Our Story

Why We Chose to Write Our Story

Budding entrepreneurs certainly read and learn from success stories. That goes without saying. And which is the reason why the business shelves of bookstores are filled with stories of GE, Dell, Amazon, E-bay, Microsoft and many others. These are the stories that inspire people to the path of entrepreneurship. And rightly so. Yet, it is only a very tiny fraction of these budding entrepreneurs, who actually emulate the success stories of such inspiring idols.

What goes wrong in such cases? Could many stories be similar to ours?

We had some genuinely great ideas. We had tons of passion, conviction, and certainly patience. We learnt well, we executed well, we built a decent team, and we raised the money. We read Drucker, Jim Collins and C.K. Prahalads. We tracked Amazon and E-bay and Yahoo and Google to see what they were doing. We did all that. Yet there was somewhere the proverbial slip between the cup and the lip.

Many entrepreneurs are likely to go astray or fall into certain traps, much like we did. Many entrepreneurs are likely to get into situations similar to ours. The wisdom that we got in hindsight could be useful to them, in such cases, as they continue to build companies.

We know that if we had to do it again, we would do a few things differently. With the wisdom and the learning we had gained in hindsight, we would be better equipped to build a successful business in the future.

We wanted to share this wisdom with other entrepreneurs. For, in their success, we will see shades of our success!

Sanjay Mehta
June 2015

Hareesh Tibrewala
June 2015

Acknowledgement

The story of Homeindia.com is the story of our lives, spanning a decade. And when a story spans a decade, lots of people become a part of the story, and end up playing a very important role in the story, even though they may not stand out in the star-cast.

Perhaps the biggest role, behind the scenes, is played by the family. As entrepreneurs, we enjoy and relish every minute of what we are doing. We are driven by a sense of mission and by passion. However, it is the immediate family that bears the brunt of our enthusiasm. Their joys and creature comforts become sub-ordinate to our entrepreneurial mission. Hence a big "THANK YOU" to our family members, our parents, our wives and our kids, for standing besides us through times good, and not-so-good, and for having faith in us.

We would also like to thank all our team members who worked at Homeindia during its decade long journey. While as entrepreneurs we bring a vision to the organisation, it is really the employees, with their functional knowledge and domain skills, who convert that vision into reality. Also, a big thanks to our investors who never lost faith in us. As your see repeatedly in this story, every time we needed any kind of support, they were there to help us.

We are also grateful to our business associates, vendors, partners, friends and well-wishes who provided support and encouragement, right through the journey.

And finally and most importantly, the biggest acknowledgement is reserved for our friend, philosopher and guide, Jayendra Shah. We met Jayendrabhai almost by accident. But that accident, re-scripted the Homeindia story. He believed in Homeindia.com as much as we did. And most of all, believed in us! In our lives, he has played the role of Krishna, the charioteer guiding us Arjunas as we fought

Sanjay Mehta and Hareesh Tibrewala

Table of Contents

PART III - 2005-2007 – The Last Mile

Prologue

The Accidental Road to Internet Entrepreneurship

"We don't write destinies. Destinies write us."

If it wasn't destiny, then what would one call that phone call from me, Hareesh Tibrewala, to Sanjay Mehta on that wintry afternoon of 1996 – a call that was going to change our lives forever.

The Phone Call

The call was like a gentle breeze that carries the pollen from the flower to its place of germination, little knowing the life-creating cause that it has achieved. I was calling Sanjay to inform him that our common friend Ajay Sevak, from the US, was visiting India and whether we could all meet up for dinner. Calendars were less complex those days and soon we zeroed down on a convenient slot. We were looking forward to it as we were all meeting after a long time.

The dinner turned out to be an eventful one.

A Little into the Past

Before getting into the details about the dinner, here is a quick backdrop. Post our Electrical Engineering from VJTI, University of Mumbai, both Sanjay and I did our M.S. from the University of Southern California in the US in 1986. Thereafter, I spent a few months in Germany and Sanjay continued to be in the US, getting trained in some companies before we both returned to India. Quite against the trend, if I may say so, where usually anyone who went to study abroad those days would eventually settle down there.

However, we had our calling in our family businesses and were soon immersed in them. Then life took its own course - both of us found our respective better halves, got married, had children, got more involved in our businesses, and life simply got busier. We were lucky to meet up once or twice a year, usually when some other friends from the US were visiting India. Yet, this did not impact our long standing friendship and whenever we met, we were able to take off from where we had left. Perhaps our days at the engineering college, our struggles through the examinations and assignments, and our days spent together while studying in the US had forged a bond that time could not weaken.

An Eventful Dinner

Coming back, the dinner was filled with reminiscences. As we kept going down the memory lane, both Sanjay and I were reminded of the passion that we both carried to tap new potential and explore exciting opportunities never sought before. We were happy in our

 If I Had To Do It Again...
The Accidental Road to Internet Entrepreneurship

daily lives but there was an undying eagerness to do something more, something beyond.

Dwelling more on this, I mentioned that I had a vacant factory space in Andheri and instead of starting a factory, which may not be very cost-effective in a city like Mumbai, I was considering some education-based initiative.

Sanjay too had few ideas in the education space. As he was running an Electrical and Electronics Engineering business, he had always noticed that advertisements for vacancies would generate a large number of applicants but there would hardly be anyone suitable for the job. This implied that on one hand, there was huge unemployment where people were desperately looking for jobs, while on the other hand, the education and training received by them did not make them competent enough for the jobs. Sanjay figured that with some additional training, we could easily convert this large pool of manpower to become more suitable for apt jobs.

As we discussed further, the waiter got us our food. Over delicious *parathas* and *dum-aloos*, we both decided that we should take this conversation forward and see if we could work together and explore opportunities in the education sector, as a new business opportunity.

That was a seed laid.

Many conversations of this nature take place but then people go back to their respective busy lives and everything is forgotten. But this one was meant to be different, which is why we met after a few days to discuss our ideas further.

Giving shape to our ideas

The first decision we took was that we would not exit from our family businesses but we would begin by investing few hours everyday to nurture our ideas.

Education was the sector we zeroed upon but were not sure of what exactly to do. Like for instance, Sanjay's idea of providing skill training to basic graduates so that they become suitable for jobs led to numerous questions - which course, what skill and the like.

We realised we had to do a thorough research before we came to a conclusion. We began meeting people and sharing our ideas with them to check their response. Finally, two business ideas were shortlisted. As is typical of many

entrepreneurial ventures, we started with a thought somewhere and ended up doing something that was quite different from that initial thought.

Business Idea - 1

Our first idea was to import professional, animated educational CDs from the US and introduce them to the children in India, with a view to providing a fun element in their education. Basically, make a child's education more interesting and fun-filled, via colourful, animated courseware. We went ahead with this idea and began operations at a small office that I had to spare in Tardeo.

If I Had To Do It Again…
The Accidental Road to Internet Entrepreneurship

Business Idea - 2

The other idea was to create education material related to the Internet. As Internet had just made its entry into India, we felt that there would be a huge need for people to get a deeper understanding of the space and find ways in which they could exploit it for their benefit. We decided to pursue this idea as well.

Deciding on Nomenclatures

The next step was to name our company. Considering the multimedia content that we would use for the children's education and the Internet seminars that we would conduct, we came up with a company name called "Multinet Systems" (not very imaginative!). When we converted it to a private limited company, we extended the name to Multinet Infosys Private Limited.

The children's education business, being a consumer brand, had to have a decent name of its own. We decided on Fun-N-Learn. Later on, when we came up with the Internet education part, we would give that also a separate brand name.

Between 1996 and 1997, we experimented with Fun-N -Learn. We were the pioneers to bring fun element into children's education. As fate would have it, we did not get it right. Perhaps the model was not correct or perhaps the marketing did not have the required glitz, the business of teaching with these educational CDs failed to get the required traction.

But in all this, we did manage to put together a strategy for our Internet education segment and were ready to roll.

And the rest, as they say, is history…

The Wisdom Nugget

> ➢ It is said that "We don't write destinies. It is destinies that write us." The story of HomeIndia.com is a story that was destined to happen. An un-planned meeting, a casual chat and an entrepreneur's spirit waiting to manifest itself. Sometimes we need to allow destiny to take its own course. Flow with the flow … and you will be surprised where it can lead you to.

If I Had To Do It Again…
The Accidental Road to Internet Entrepreneurship

PART I

1996-2000 :
The Wonder Years

The journey started in 1996, when the Internet was still not being hyped about and words like 'Dotcom Boom' were still not heard of. In that sense, we did not get into this business because we "saw" the boom. We got in because we saw the opportunity.

Within a year of being in the business, exciting stuff started happening in the Internet space, which included big IPOs of dotcom companies in the US and some mind-blowing acquisitions.

We pretty much found ourselves in the high tides of the dotcom boom. Media wanted to talk to us, advertisers wanted to work with us, awesome talent wanted their share of the dotcom experience, investors wanted their share of the dotcom pie… all in all, it was an exciting period!

Those were clearly the heady days. When nothing could go wrong, or so it seemed. No wonder then that we refer to this period as 'The Wonder Years.'

Chapter 1

Internet Express Seminars

Bootstrapping the Business

When we decided on the education sector for our business, one of the persons we called upon was Ketan Sanghvi.

Ketan was another good friend of ours from the US. He had completed his B.S. and MBA from the University of Southern California and had briefly taken up few assignments in the US thereafter. However like us, he too had decided to come back to India to take care of his family business.

We had kept in touch with Ketan and we both agreed that he would be an apt person to seek an opinion from. At that point, we were trying to zero down on the specific courses in the education space that we could focus on.

Though Ketan's family was into textile machinery manufacturing, he, out of his own interest had ventured into the technology space. Internet was just making its way into India and seizing the opportunity, Ketan had set up a firm that dealt with marketing of communication equipments, such as modems, to companies in India. In fact, he represented one of the leading brands in this line of business – ZyXel.

Being a techie at heart, he loved to dabble in this space and always got into deep conversations with his clients and prospects about connectivity and communication matters. Due to this penchant, Ketan often met lot of people who, in those early years of Internet in India, were striving to get their businesses online.

When we approached him, true to our beliefs, Ketan suggested a brilliant idea. Most of the people in India were curious to know what the Internet was all about and they were constantly seeking someone to know more about it. So, how about a course on Internet?

We looked at each other, smiled and thought why not!

But there was a small problem. While we had used email networks during our student days, we did not carry the expertise of teaching people. We needed experts in this space. And as the Internet space was new, experts would be few.

Here again, Ketan came to our rescue. Searching through his contacts, he gave us the name of a person whom we could speak to.

The person was an M.Tech from IIT, Mumbai and was working at one of the very few Internet based businesses in India at that point of time - Ravi Database Co.. This company was owned by Rajesh Jain, one of the earliest Internet entrepreneurs in India. The company created and managed well-known properties like Indiaworld.com, Khoj.com, Samachar.com and many others. The person whom Ketan wanted us to meet was the key technology person in that company. He felt that it would be an interesting meeting, if nothing else. That was how we ended up meeting Shuvam Misra for the first time.

  If I Had To Do It Again…
    Bootstrapping the Business

Shuvam wanted to hear us out first – our idea and our intention. After listening to us, he was impressed enough to participate.

A person who would completely understand the perspectives of a situation before sharing his thoughts, Shuvam agreed that there was ample room to evangelize the Internet.

He had a clear understanding about the Internet space and would have featured in the list of top 20-25 Internet experts in India at that point of time. We were lucky to get in touch with him and soon developed a mutual liking for each other.

From three friends, we became four. We were so excited about the concept that we had immense fun laying out the details. We all agreed that we should exceed the market expectation in terms of sharing knowledge about the Internet.

While both of us were looking at this project to be our business launch, for Ketan and Shuvam, it was as much about being able to evangelize the Internet as about making some money.

In such a scenario, we agreed upon a Memorandum of Understanding (MoU) among us. The broad points of the MoU were:

- All four of us would put in intellectual capital into the project and will be treated as equal participants.

- The infrastructure and the investment would be raised from the company that we had set up. The company would be the fifth 'participant' in a broader sense.

- The gross profits would be divided among the five entities.

There, the MoU was done.

Perhaps, it was the passion we had in the project that enabled us to quickly come to a consensus over the MoU. Or else, in some cases, figuring out the terms of such an MoU could become the reason for business ventures not taking off, where participants would lock horns over certain clauses.

We had another informal agreement. Since Ketan was in the business of selling modems, we decided that we would use only his modems for all our business activities. If opportunities arose to promote modems, we would be promoting only those modems sold by Ketan's company.

Developing the Business Model

With the MoU in place, we now forayed into the business development phase of the project.

Deciding the Target Audience

We had to decide our target audience for whom we would design the courseware. We came to a conclusion that it would be working professionals, corporate executives and business owners. We felt they would be the ones who needed knowledge of this kind the most, and would also be willing to spend money to get educated.

 | If I Had To Do It Again…
Bootstrapping the Business

Deciding the Format of the Course

As it was meant for working professionals, we decided on seminars instead of long duration courses that we would have otherwise planned, if we were targeting, say students. A day-long seminar at a five star hotel, where participants would be given enriching knowledge about the Internet and where they could network with other like-minded people over refreshments or lunch, sounded like a perfect plan.

Deciding the Content

As the content was being developed, we were all learning several aspects about the computer and the Internet alike. For instance, we had not done much work on Powerpoint earlier. But now the seminar content was in the form of a presentation. So, we learnt how to use apt backgrounds and text colours so that they stood out when projected in the dark or how to use transitions and custom animations or ensuring that the slides had only bullet points and not long paragraphs, so that the participants focused on the speaker rather than the slides.

Everyone of us worked on the slides, but the main architect was clearly Shuvam. The first set of content that we got together had interesting topics that would stretch through an entire day. That was fine with us. After all, a day-long seminar would ensure that participants got back decent value for their money.

Over time, as we would get feedback from the participants, we would incorporate them into the content, enhancing it further.

Branding the Seminar

We now had to decide on a name for our programme. "The Internet Seminar" or "A Seminar about the Internet" sounded boring. Moreover, we were creating a 'product,' so it had to be aptly branded. After some discussion and debate, we zeroed down on the name "Internet Express" – meaning a quick (express) introduction to the Internet.

Hosting the Seminar

After finalising the name, it was time to find a venue. Our first thought was five-star hotels. However, after working out the costs, we realised that if we had to make it a cash-positive event, we would have to charge Rs 4,000 per participant. That sounded too much money in 1996 and none of us were confident that we would get a decent participant-base at this cost. We began looking for alternatives - three-star hotels, banquet halls and similar venues.

We also had to come to a decision on few issues like the occurrence of the seminar – one a day or more than one? How do we showcase the presentation slides to the participants? How do we advertise ourselves and finally how do we collect money from the participants?

After a lot of thought and planning, we came up with these points:

- o Mumbai being a large city, people may not travel long distances, even if it was an attractive event. Hence, we decided to launch with two seminars - spaced a week apart from each other. One was to be held in the suburbs, and the

 If I Had To Do It Again…
Bootstrapping the Business

other in South Mumbai, closer to the business districts. For the venue, we zeroed down on Hotel Atithi near Santacruz airport as our first location and the World Trade Center at Cuffe Parade as our second location. We scheduled the first event for Saturday, March 23, 1996 and the second one for the subsequent Saturday, March 30, 1996. We decided to charge Rs 1500 per participant for a full day event.

- To get the word out about the seminar, we thought of putting a decent sized advertisement in the Economic Times, as the readers were definitely our target audience. This was to be our first fixed cost. We decided to use the same advertisement to promote both the events. This, we felt, would give us a chance to recover our fixed cost and also give us a better opportunity to make more money. We also planned to offer early bird discounts, group discounts for more than one participant from the same company and other such incentives that are typical for events of this kind.

- We decided to rent out an OHP (Overhead projector) and a screen, and the computer through which we would showcase the presentation. That became our second fixed cost.

Pre-Registrations

Pre-registrations started trickling in. Considering that it was our first seminar, it was exciting. However, the registrations were not large in numbers. That had us all anxious. We pinned our hopes on the on-the-spot registrations that we had kept open. We were anxious and were constantly wondering how many people would show up on the first day of the seminar. With this anxiety, we got ready for Day One.

All Set for Day One

While Shuvam and Ketan were far more experienced in the Internet space, we decided that all four of us would take part in the seminar and present parts of the content. We did our homework thoroughly. We hired the OHP in advance to see how the screen appeared. We fine-tuned the presentation to make it crisper.

As we were to rent the PC through which we would project the content, we had to copy the presentation on a 3.25" floppy disk. We copied it onto the first floppy and, as a backup, made a second copy. However, Shuvam insisted we make eight to ten copies. Eight to ten copies? Whoever had heard of this kind of a backup? Yet we complied. We also took paper and transparency prints of the slides, just in case. Ketan was ready with the modem and connectivity equipments. We were all prepared.

We all decided to wear suits. After all, we had to look impressive and make the right impact as Internet experts.

And so dawned Day One.

Day One: March 23, 1996, Our First Seminar

We all reached Hotel Atithi well in advance and got going with the set-up. The OHP was connected and the floppy worked fine. Internet connectivity, during those times, was highly unreliable but

If I Had To Do It Again…
Bootstrapping the Business

we managed to dial out and Ketan was confident that we had a good connection.

With the set up done, we waited anxiously for the on-the-spot registrations. And they came. In small trickle at the beginning, till a point where we had a near full house. A few relatives and friends were present to boost our morale, but other than them, all the 60 seats were fully paid. We were happy. We had already recovered the cost of the ET ad and the OHP rental. The money we would generate from the second event would be our profit.

The seminar went off extremely well and was well received by the audience. With strong focus on ensuring value for money to the participants, we went to lengths to respond to each and every query. The participants went back a satisfied lot and our survey form that they filled after the seminar showed excellent feedback.

At the end of the day, we realised that we were onto something interesting. Our suit pockets bulging with cash were additional proof, if any was needed!

Day Two: March 30, 1996, Our Second Seminar

The venue was the World Trade Center in South Mumbai, where many businesses had their base. Although the first seminar was a success, we were a little tensed about this one. Perhaps, we were expecting a bigger audience and a more discerning one.

As usual, we reached the venue well in advance and went about with the set-up. We switched on the computer, connected the OHP and inserted the floppy that contained the presentation. It failed to work. We were unperturbed, after all we had seven floppies as backup. We inserted the second one, then the third one, then the fourth one…none worked. We were losing count of the floppies and were frantically thinking of plan B. Seven floppies had refused to work, was our second seminar destined to be through paper prints and transparencies? We were now inserting the eighth floppy. Where seven had not worked, would the eighth stand a chance? And believe you me, it worked. Our collective relieved sighs were, perhaps, heard outside. That was the time when immense and profound respect welled up within all of us for Shuvam, who had recommended several backup copies. He knew about the reliability challenges that floppies faced during those times and had prepared us accordingly. That is what being an expert is all about, we realised.

With the set-up done, we waited for the on-the-spot registrations. The World Trade Center hall has a capacity of nearly 120 persons. We had about 40 pre-registrations. We hoped for another 20 to 30 participants at least, so as to surpass the first seminar.

People started walking in and the registrations shot up to 100. It was a thrilling experience and we celebrated that evening.

Through the two seminars, we had generated decent money. We had delivered good content. We had created an early reputation of sorts and people were talking about us. We both agreed that we actually were onto something big and planned to do many more seminars following this one.

Internet Express was on! We needed to take it far and wide now.

And we did so in the next two years.

Growing Internet Express

We began to conduct events with just the two of us, instead of four. Considering their expertise, initially we had ensured that either Shuvam or Ketan was with one of us. However, over time as both of us developed greater understanding of the Internet space, it did not matter which two of us were conducting the seminars. This enabled us to do many more events.

There were phases when pre-registrations would be really small. That had us worried and we would put up an additional advertisement in ET just to try and cover the ground. That, in turn, would hurt our margins, but it was important that we kept having full houses.

Tie-Up with Industrial Bodies

In order to ensure that we are able conduct such events on a regular basis and to

hedge our own risks to a certain extent, we tied up with many industry bodies for regular events. We worked with the Indian Merchants' Chamber, the Indo

American Society, the Bombay Chartered Accountants' Society and other such associations.

With these tie-ups, we always had a nearly-guaranteed audience without any advertisements. We did not have to book halls either. However, what we did was compromise on our earnings, but that did not matter because we managed to keep building the Internet Express brand. We also generated goodwill for ourselves, created a perception in the marketplace that we were "the Internet experts" and got a fair amount of rub-off benefits.

Curiosity Generates Queries

At the end of each event, a fair number of participants would walk up to us to enquire about the next steps of their Internet journey:

- How to set up a website for their business or

- Getting Internet set-up done at their offices and training their people

Initially, we took these queries as referral opportunities. Over time though, we developed our own services in both of these areas.

We set up a website development company and ended up building the first website for some of the marquee brands and companies in India - like Indian Rayon, Camlin, Wockhardt, L&T Finance, and many others. We built a small team of six to seven people for this service.

We also offered the service of selling modems to companies and training their office staff, in order to get them started on using email and Internet. We had a small team of one to two people for this purpose and made decent money out of it.

If I Had To Do It Again…
Bootstrapping the Business

Both services were direct offshoots of the seminars that we did. The more events that we conducted, the more the leads poured in. What was even more interesting was that the clients saw us as experts rather than vendors, enabling us to get a small premium over competition. And no, we did not have to market ourselves at all for these services.

Looking Back at Our Bootstrapping Techniques

When we started the business, we had decided that we would not take any significant capital from our family business. We did utilize some spare office space though, which was to be returned once we had our own independent space. By not taking any capital from the family business, we had pushed ourselves to the edge and had to clearly bootstrap the business. With the seminars, we managed to do a great job of bootstrapping. Here is how -

When we advertised for our seminars in newspapers, we got a reasonable credit period to pay for these advertisements. Similarly, the banquet hall, the computer and OHP providers also had to be paid at the end of the seminars. This meant that all our expenses were on credit.

As we collected cash-in-advance from the participants, we paid all our vendors through our earnings itself. What remained after our expenses was our gross profit. This way, we began our seminars with zero budget. The profits went into a reserve and when we had sufficient money, we picked up our first computer and a specialised carry bag for the same. Remember, we are not talking about compact laptops but a full-fledged computer with a large monitor, a big PC unit, keyboard, mouse, wires, etc. This was what we carried around for all of our events. And which was why, we got a special bag made that would hold all these items securely through our many journeys on bumpy roads in the city.

Later, when our modem and email set up services began to gain momentum, we hired our first employee to cater to these services. When more money poured in, we bought more machines and brought on board our first two web designers.

We expanded our office layout by taking over some more space that our family business had to spare in Dadar and Tardeo.

With all this, we were up and running. Our startup was launched. At a low cost, we had got going.

We adapted and then adapted some more. Now, we needed to scale up and we could be in for a great future.

Would that happen? Or would destiny have something else in mind for us?

The Wisdom Nugget

- An entrepreneur does not need to be a 'domain' expert. He usually is someone who sees an opportunity and is able to 'learn' his way through to make it happen.

- We all have access to a huge network of friends and acquaintances. Learn to make use of that network when building a start-up. Lot of our friends and well wishers will

If I Had To Do It Again…
Bootstrapping the Business

be more than willing to guide us in areas where we need help. Hence, we should make optimum use of this 'friendship capital.'

➤ More start-ups die because they run out of cash, than for any other reason! Keeping cash flows under control and ensuring that there is enough money in the bank to pay the bills is of prime importance.

Chapter 2

From VDIS to Online Post

Three Cheers to HomeIndia.com

The first phase of our business had got going. We were conducting seminars, building websites and providing e-mail and modem services to people at their offices. While we created the first website for some of the top companies in India, we felt it would be a good idea to book our own domain name and perhaps develop a website.

In those times, websites were a luxury and not everyone had them, except for few companies with an international focus like an export company, for example. People may have had e-mail IDs but websites were developed after much thought and consideration, unlike today where every business or company has a website. It was so because first, it was costly and second, people wondered if they actually needed it.

We also wondered. Did we really need a website? If yes, what would be its purpose and who would it be used for? We were a service-oriented business targeting Indian audience, who had little or no access to websites due to extremely low penetration of the Internet.

Even if we built a website, it would not reach out to our target audience. Moreover, the name of the company also did not support this idea - imagine www.MultiNetSystemsPvtLtd.com. Phew! No, there was no need for our company to have a website, unless we were providing some services to the Indians residing out of India – the Non-Resident Indians (NRIs).

Birth of HomeIndia.com

NRIs have always been on our mind. Having stayed abroad, we understood how much they missed their home in India. What if we could provide them some services that would bring them closer to home? With this thought in mind, we began searching for a domain name and came across an apt one - HomeIndia. We booked it straight away.

We were yet to decide on the services for the NRIs, but having booked the domain name, we tried our hand at making the website. We are talking about 1997-98, when Netscape browsers were very famous. Netscape is what is known today as Firefox. Within the browser, Netscape had an extension of editor tools so that you could create an HTML page and view it too. So one Sunday afternoon, using the Netscape editor, we created the first look of the website. It was funny because we randomly developed something and passed it off as the website's first look. Nevertheless, that was how www. homeindia.com was born.

HomeIndia.com Gains Traction

For the next few days, we kept thinking about the content that could be put up on the website. We began by uploading information about our company, the seminars we hosted, the details of our clients, and the like. It soon became a website exhibiting the details of our company, except that it was called HomeIndia instead of Multinet India. Occasionally, we put up random stuff. Apart from that, nothing much was happening on the website. But we always knew there was a scope to do more.

We soon stumbled upon one such opportunity.

The then Finance Minister, Mr. P. Chidambaram had announced a Voluntary Disclosure of Income Scheme (VDIS) for taxpayers. The scheme aimed at converting black money into white. The only thing that a person had to do was to

declare his income, pay a certain amount of money and then the money would be his, "officially." It was a major anti-black-money-laundering scheme and attracted a

lot of people. At the same time, there were several queries and concerns around the topic and many people wished to understand the scheme better.

We pondered on whether we could answer these queries. Of course, we neither had the authority nor the knowledge to answer them. So, we decided to create an online forum, where people could post their queries and a panel of experts could answer them. The panel would comprise mainly of Chartered Accountants and similar

If I Had To Do It Again…
Three Cheers to HomeIndia.com

professionals and the queries would be posted, where else, but on HomeIndia.com. It sounded like a brilliant idea and we soon put together our panel of experts. You could say that it was sort of a social media initiative, way ahead of its time. Being a collaborative effort, it worked very well. We received lot of queries. We even had the honour of meeting the Finance Minister who liked and appreciated our concept and inaugurated the forum by clicking on a button. It was actually a high point that the Finance Minister was visiting our website, that too in its initial days. All the queries that were posted on the forum were answered by the panel. It was indeed a success. The VDIS activity actually got the website its first traction.

Beginning of a Game-Changer

Life continued. The website also continued running at its own pace through regular updates about VDIS and our services. In the mean time, a very interesting event took place, which became a game-changer for us.

Mr. Sabeer Bhatia, an Indian entrepreneur in the US, was in the news for having sold Hotmail (webmail service) to Microsoft at a whopping USD 400 million. It was 'the' news then because it was for the first time that a young Indian entrepreneur in a new-age Internet business had created a product that attracted this huge a valuation. The fact that it was an Internet business and that we were already in that space made it all the more fascinating for us.

We were intrigued by the idea that an Internet business started by an Indian somewhere in the world could have had such a big global impact. We were inspired and began exploring the Internet space further. We brainstormed on what more could be done and whether we could draw any learning from this deal.

We analysed Hotmail and concluded that its success lay embedded in the people's need to communicate.

Prior to Hotmail, one had access to e-mail services only at the office or the University. However, once they stepped out of these premises, they would lose the access. It is this gap that Hotmail had addressed. With Hotmail, people, especially in the US, were able to access e-mail through the browser and such a browser was easily available if one had a computer and Internet connectivity. Hotmail was the first browser-based e-mail and thus managed to attract a huge user base. We also reckoned that no advertisements would have gone in publicising Hotmail. Rather, all the publicity might have been viral, where one would have recommended it to another, and people started adopting Hotmail organically, but rapidly.

The reason behind Hotmail's success, we concluded, was the need for people to stay in touch, to communicate with one another – be it friends, family or colleagues. This was the learning we took.

Birth of Online Post Service

However, we did not see the necessity or relevance to create an Indian Hotmail, because the Indian user base on the Internet was abysmally low at that point. Creating a platform just to connect a handful of people did not make sense. Was there any other way we could make use of this learning?

Slowly, it dawned on us that there was a considerable number of Indians residing abroad – be it for studies, business or for jobs, and most of them had access to computer and Internet - at least those who were based in North America. They would love to keep in touch with their family and friends in India. But the only catch was that their folks back home did not have access to the computer and Internet.

How do we bridge this gap between these two groups? How do we get both of them to communicate? Communicating abroad and vice versa was an expensive affair at that point of time and no low-cost solution was in vicinity. Moreover, a typical letter took a long time to reach (roughly about 15 days). The entire back and forth cycle of communication was slow, tedious and definitely not cheap. That was when we thought of a service called Online Post.

Here is how the service would work - an NRI with Internet connectivity would log

onto HomeIndia.com and click on Online Post service. It would take him to a message box, where he would type the intended recipient's postal address and then the actual message, and click on Submit. Once submitted, the HomeIndia team would receive an e-mail. The e-mail would be processed through a software and the message would be formatted suitably. The message would then be printed out, put into an envelope and physically mailed out via Indian Post to the recipient.

We were utilising the power of the Internet, which had still not reached most Indian households then, to create this online postal service. We felt elated.

Another inspiration taken from Hotmail was that the service had to be free of cost. Hotmail was free and it generated revenue through advertisements.

We adopted that model and decided to offer the postal service for free and generate our revenue through online advertisements. While the only serious expense that Hotmail incurred as it moved millions of messages back and forth, was the bandwidth cost, we had to bear the expense of printing the messages and sending them out via post. This included cost of paper, cartridge for printing, envelope, postage stamps, and of course, the effort of the people in processing these letters. Apart from the expenses, it was a daunting task to ensure that all the messages reached the right recipient and in reasonable time too.

Nevertheless, we decided to go ahead because we realised that 'free' was the only way to make this service successful. Just a reminder that this service was happening alongside our other lines of businesses, viz. conducting seminars and building websites.

We went ahead and created the platform. Since, we did not have any marketing budget, we simply sent out e-mails to about 20 to 30 friends in the US intimating

them about the Online Post service that we had launched. This was the only so-called "launch" that we did. By the end of the first week, we received about 10 to 20 letters per day. Not bad to start off with. However, as the weeks progressed, the frequency of the letters increased and by the end of the month, we were receiving close to 500 to 1000 letters per day. That was indeed a very huge number and that our service had gone viral was there for everyone to see. By the end of three months, we were receiving about 3000 letters a day.

Every single day, 3000 letters were being printed and posted. Our office had literally turned into a mini post office. While Hotmail would have had only bits and bytes flowing as part of their service, our service involved physical, printed letters that were filled with heartfelt emotions, which most of the times seemed to flow endlessly as the NRIs got in touch with their folks back home. We respected the emotions and did our best to ensure that the messages were delivered at the earliest to the recipients. Each and every letter was important. Each and every letter had to be delivered. We did not have the luxury of saying that we were able to deliver only 90 to 95 percent of the letters. With this in mind, we put lot of checks and controls in place that enabled us to manage 100 percent successful deliveries everyday.

However, beyond a point, it was getting very difficult to handle all the posts internally. We began to look for a potential company to whom we could outsource the envelope preparation and the mailing activity. This meant incurring extra costs but that was the only way out to ensure that all the letters reached the recipients within the stipulated time.

After the outsourcing initiative, the service started running very smoothly. We were happy but one thought kept nagging us. Right now our service enabled the NRIs to reach out to people in India, but what if the recipients in India, who did not have access to the Internet, wanted to respond? Could we enable that as well? After all, communication works well only when it is two-way.

Enabling Two-Way Communication

With this thought in mind, we created a 'reverse communication process.' What we did was that, along with the message, we began to send an intimation, enquiring if the recipient wanted to write back to the NRI, and also a form where they could write or type their letter on to. We also asked them to share the NRI's e-mail ID with us. We then created an inbox for the NRI on HomeIndia.com, scanned the letter and uploaded it onto his or her inbox through a software. The NRI could then logon to the website anytime and check the message.

This had the NRIs coming back to the website to check if there were any mails waiting for them. Where initially they came only to post the messages, now they were logging in to check for incoming mails. With this initiative, we managed two things - first to establish a two-way communication process, and second, to increase the footfalls on our website. Increased footfalls eventually led to an increase in advertising revenue, with more advertisers showing their interest to showcase their products and services on our website.

Meanwhile, there were many advertisers who wanted to reach out to the Indian audience. The letters sent by the NRIs made for the perfect targeting of such people. So, as part of our revenue strategy, along with the letters that got

If I Had To Do It Again…
Three Cheers to HomeIndia.com

delivered, we began including pamphlets and flyers of the advertisers who wanted to reach out to "resident Indians who had close connections with the NRIs."

With this, we had initiated a two-way advertising. While on the website, we had advertisers who wanted to reach out to the NRIs (like banks that focused on NRI customers, for example); in the letters that we posted, we had advertisers who wanted to reach out to the Indian audience (like cross-border money transfer service providers, for example). This, in turn, led to a two-way revenue generation.

Never Thought of Before – Online Gifting

As the business progressed, another thought hit us. The NRI had been sending letters to India, and as it was a free service, he was doing it twice or thrice a week. Since he was showing so much interest, there must be some meaningful bond or relationship between him and the recipients. Then, how would he like it if he could do something special for them during their birthdays or on other important occasions? We realised that he would love it. The next thought then was - can a person sitting in Chicago be able to send a gift to his family in Surat or Ahmedabad or Chennai or Jalandhar? Could we actually enable it? The thought was exciting because sending gifts abroad and vice versa was a mammoth and expensive process those days.

We decided to enable it and put up a gift shop on HomeIndia.com, along with the Online Post service. The gifts included products like bouquets, cakes and other such items. The service was offered mainly to the NRIs and we put up a banner saying that these products could be delivered to their families in India. A payment gateway was set up and all that the NRIs had to do was log on to the website, select the gift and click on the payment option. All the payments were to be made in dollars. Soon, gifting became an extension to our Online Post service.

An interesting insight into this whole initiative was that with the gifting option, we were targeting the same audience who were coming to the site to avail free service. Free service was the draw, while this paid offering generated for us the revenue.

As we were already handling a sensitive part of sending their letters to their folks in India and doing it well, the NRIs had built a trust in us. Now, they trusted that we would deliver their gifts too. Hence, based on the trust, we were able to entice free-service customers to use our paid services. During those times, it was indeed a challenge to get someone to use their credit card and make online payment, especially for gifting purposes. Risk of fraud and theft loomed large and sending gifts via mail or courier was always a risk. But since we had established the trust, it was easy for us to ask them to trust us further with the gifting. Or else, it would have been difficult to get traction for a gift store, if that was the core business we had started out with. Establishing trust helped us diversify smoothly.

We now had a decent business running. HomeIndia.com had taken off!

 | If I Had To Do It Again…
Three Cheers to HomeIndia.com

The Wisdom Nugget

- ➤ "Entrepreneurship is about 99 percent perspiration and one percent inspiration." However we must realise that, that the 'one' percent inspiration plays an important part in making a person a 100 percent entrepreneur. So, allow yourself to be inspired. Soak in the inputs from various sources, from success stories, from other entrepreneurial journeys, from biographies, from stories of innovation in various fields, etc. There will be a learning in all those and you will typically find value at various points in your own entrepreneurial journey.

- ➤ Focus on building 'value.' Find a problem to solve. And if you want to build a big solution, find a big problem. Online Post (and later Online Gifting) was an example of a solution that addressed real problems, and thus became an instant success.

Chapter 3

The India Internet Awards

Beyond the 15 Seconds of Fame!

The business had taken off very well. Our Online Gifting segment was as popular as our Online Post service and we were growing reasonably well.

It was around this time that we saw an advertisement in the business daily - The Economic Times. The advertisement announced a set of Internet Awards, the first of its kind in India. The year was 1998, when Internet was just making its foray into India and to have a national award in that space sounded exciting.

We checked out the categories to see where we would fit. There were many, such as - the Most Popular Website, Best Looking Website, etc. But the one that stood out and attracted our attention was the category – the Most Useful Website.

We thought HomeIndia.com fitted well in that category. After all, the Online Post and Online Gifting services were doing a fantastic job of connecting NRIs to their families, friends and relatives. It certainly was a useful website. We decided to apply for it and felt we stood a very good chance of winning. The only catch was that there was no jury and it was the online users who would nominate the websites and vote the winners.

Garnering Visibility for HomeIndia.com

We had not invested much in marketing or advertisements, so within India HomeIndia.com was not well known. The Internet properties were considered to be niche at that point of time. Having said that, sites like RediffOnTheNet (what is today known as Rediff.com), Indiaworld.com and Samachar.com (a news aggregation site) had managed to make some right noises and were visible and popular among the people. Compared to these, HomeIndia.com had very low visibility.

We had to increase our visibility. But how? We decided to put up a banner next to Online Post service saying, "If you find this website to be useful, do vote for us by clicking here." When they clicked, it took them to the voting page, where details of the awards were mentioned. This was the only effort we took as far as marketing ourselves was concerned. We simply had no idea how many people would be voting for us. But considering that we were receiving thousands of letters every day, some people would definitely be voting. The voting process was supposed to run for few weeks. We kept our fingers crossed.

Taking Part in the Award Ceremony

The award ceremony was taking place in Delhi in conjunction with an event, rather an exhibition - the India Internet World. It was the Indian version of the global event - Internet World. Considering it was taking place in Pragati Maidan, the largest exhibition centre in Delhi, it was going to be a huge event. We see events of such scale happening now, but back in 1998 it was a big deal. Sanjay decided to go to Delhi, more so with an intention of attending the event.

The exhibition was spread over a couple of days, so he took ample time to visit and explore all the booths. Then came the awards night, which was taking place at a five-star hotel. Sanjay had spent the day at the exhibition and towards the evening, set out for the ceremony. He had clearly underestimated the Delhi traffic and reached just in time as the awards were to be announced. The hall was full and only the seats at the back were available. He quickly seated himself.

The award ceremony was taking place in a true Oscar / Filmfare fashion. The winners' names remained sealed in envelopes and various celebrities were being called upon the stage to open the envelopes, announce the winners and hand over the awards to them.

The 15 Seconds of Fame

Soon, it was time for the Most Useful Website category. And guess the celebrity who was called on the stage to give away this award - the poster boy of Internet, founder of Hotmail.com that had been acquired by Microsoft for a whooping USD 400 million, the inspiration behind Online Post service - Sabeer Bhatia. Sanjay could not stop smiling. Sabeer opened the envelope. Sanjay sat calmly on his

seat. Sabeer then paused and asked the audience to take some guesses. The suspense was building. Then he slowly announced the name…. and it was

HomeIndia.com. Sanjay froze on his seat. Could this be really happening? He let out a scream of exhilaration and rushed towards the stage. At that moment, he could relate to people who would jump and let out surprised screams when they would win awards. He was undergoing similar emotions, but by the time he reached the stage, he had composed himself and even managed to tell Sabeer Bhatia, in his 15 seconds of interaction with him, that he had been the inspiration behind HomeIndia.com. He was gracious enough to acknowledge. Sanjay came back to his seat still feeling on cloud nine.

Our first venture, our first award – it meant a lot.

Our Moment of Stardom

After the ceremony, Sanjay reached the hotel and called up everyone to share the big news. In an era sans live coverage, sans Whatsapp, you had to call up and inform. There was lot of excitement and everyone felt proud about the award. With that high, he retired to sleep.

Next morning, both of us started receiving a string of phone calls from friends, relatives and business acquaintances, congratulating us on the award. We were wondering how the news had reached them. The answer lay in the morning newspaper. Apparently, The Economic Times, a leading business daily, had featured a front page photograph of Sabeer Bhatia handing over the 'Most Useful Website Award' for HomeIndia.com to Sanjay. Overnight, both of us had become mini-celebrities, at least in the circle of people who knew us and in the circle of other fellow Internet entrepreneurs.

Being a Times Group event, the award ceremony was given huge coverage on the front page of both the dailies - The Economic Times and The Times Of India. In fact, the photograph was followed by a three-column story describing the event in both the papers. Since Sabeer Bhatia was in the news because of his recent success, he obviously was featured on the front page, and since Sanjay was standing with him, he featured too. Out of the eight to ten awards that were given away that evening, it was only Sanjay's photograph that got featured. That was being plain lucky.

We felt we had been very lucky, of late. If the award ceremony had not been linked to the event - India Internet World, then perhaps Sanjay would not have made the trip to Delhi. Because Sanjay went to Delhi, he took part in the award function. Considering the traffic he faced that evening, Sanjay could have very well missed the function, but he made it. And when the awards were to be handed out, the celebrity called upon had to be Sabeer Bhatia and, as if a script was unfolding, HomeInida.com won and Sanjay went to receive the award. Since he received the award from Sabeer Bhatia and was photographed at the apt moment, HomeIndia.com made it to the front page of the newspapers. Coincidences were too many.

We have always believed that when many coincidences are leading your path, it is pure destiny. And we are firm believers of destiny.

Entry of Venture Capitalists

One of the calls that came in that morning was from Vamesh Chovatia, who represented an investment banking firm. He had called up to congratulate us and to enquire if we were interested in Venture Capital (VC).

In 1998, the concept of VC was quite new. Since both of us came from traditional business backgrounds, our thought process revolved around putting our own money into the business or at the maximum, availing a loan. We had absolutely no exposure to VC. Left to ourselves, we would have found it very difficult to approach the Venture Capitalists, but with the publicity that the award gave us, the investors themselves were approaching us. Later, we got to know that on account of the dotcom boom that was happening in the West, investors were looking for interesting investment opportunities within the Indian dotcom space. And since we were the recipient of an award, they felt we were definitely doing something right in the Internet space and looked forward to getting in touch with us.

Vamesh suggested that we meet him. During our meeting, he further cleared the concept of VC to us. Meanwhile, there were other people who were contacting us. They were not direct investors but the go-between or the matchmakers between the companies that needed funding and the VCs who were looking for potential investment options.

The award definitely had opened doors to several VC options. Not to mention our enhanced popularity in the social circle, where we even began receiving letters and phone calls from unknown people who were intrigued by the Internet business and our success and wanted to know more about both.

The 15 seconds of interaction with Sabeer Bhatia, which we would term as destiny playing its part, turned out to be the biggest '15 seconds of fame' for us

and we decided to capitalise the opportunity to the maximum. Riding on the visibility and the publicity, we began exploring the VC option to our advantage to take our business to the next level.

The Wisdom Nugget

➤ As a CEO, you are your business's biggest brand ambassador. Unabashedly, leverage every opportunity to talk about your business. The 'Most Useful Website' award gave us that opportunity and we leveraged it to the fullest.

➤ "Capital" is like oxygen for a business. And if you don't have adequate oxygen, it becomes challenging for a business to grow. Be ready to raise capital using whatever means you have access to.

➤ The idea of giving equity ownership of your business is an unnerving idea. However, if it helps to grow the business, then it is absolutely worth it. Without adequate track record and without serious tangible assets (often the case in new-age businesses), it is challenging to get bank debt, and swapping equity for capital becomes the only option. In such a case, there should not be any hesitation in going this route, as what really counts is to make the pie larger, even if you have a smaller slice of that larger pie.

Chapter 4

"Money Without Collateral, but Where's My Equity?"

Enter the VC

Vamesh Chovatia was a relative and a friend of Sanjay, but interactions with him were few and far in between. However, every time we met him, we would be convinced about his uncanny knack for business. He worked with Prime Securities Ltd., a financial services company and had an excellent nose for business. He could sniff the mood of the investors and the market, and spot exactly where potential business deals lay. No wonder then that he came to meet us and check out the Online Post service, when it was launched on HomeIndia.com. He continued to keep in touch with us after that, occasionally enquiring how the business was progressing. He understood the waves that the Internet business was creating at that point of time. He even introduced us to few of his team members to understand the concept of VC better, but at that point, there were many unanswered questions and we let things be.

But now that we had won the award, Vamesh sensed that it was an opportune time for us to explore the VC option once again. The serenading media, which was giving us great publicity, further confirmed Vamesh's gut feel that HomeIndia.com was a story that had to be narrated to the Venture Capitalists.

At that point, it was not only Vamesh or the Venture Capitalists who were showing interest in our business. There were merchant bankers and several others who wanted to invest in us, and the way they were reaching out to us was, at times, overwhelming.

Like for instance, one day a person sent us a fax stating that he could help us raise a substantial amount of capital. Yet another person approached us through a family friend. Since he came via a family friend, he took it for granted that it would be he who would be raising money for us. We politely let him know that there were others we were talking to and that he could not take the mandate for granted. Then, there were others who approached us formally requesting a meeting.

There was, in particular, a renowned merchant bank head honcho who, when he

heard that his executives were not able to make headway in convincing us about the firm's credentials for the job, decided to come to our office himself. But as he was busy during the week, he requested a meeting on a Sunday morning. The pitch to a dotcom startup like us was perhaps a part of his hobby, and not formal 'work' for a big shot like him.

We were genuinely overwhelmed and decided to meet every investor. The meetings were like interviews, where we quizzed these intermediaries to judge if they suited us. It is a usual practice for a person to show off all the knowledge he has during an interview. What better opportunity for us than these interviews to learn more about an industry that we had just stepped into, to know more about our competitors and about the latest technologies that were doing rounds. From that perspective, the interactions with the merchant bankers were truly enlightening.

By the time we finished the meetings with all the investors, we had a good idea about this animal called VC. We also understood that while raising money, the selection of a merchant banker was very critical. A good choice would mean that you get a good valuation and you raise your money within a short span of time. In short, there is a kind of chemistry that brews between you and the banker, making way for a good-spirited relationship, in which things fall in place easily.

On the other hand, a wrong choice would mean disagreement in many areas, like the business plan or the overall strategy, leading to wastage of time and ultimately to a difficult marriage between the entrepreneur and the VC.

We had to make a right choice and we were not in a hurry. Not when we were being offered a choice!

We continued our interactions with the investors and finally zeroed down on the person we wanted to work with. It was Vamesh Chovatia.

 | If I Had To Do It Again…
Enter the VC

Selecting the Correct Banker

How did we zero down upon Vamesh Chovatia and Prime Securities? What are the criteria one should have in mind while selecting a merchant banker?

- First of all, the company that is proposing to help raise money for you should assign a champion for your case. The champion should be fairly senior and genuinely interested in your case, which is when you will see traction in your case. In Vamesh, we saw that champion.

- The deal must be equally interesting to the merchant banker as it is for you. If your fund requirement is too small for your merchant banker, and for some reason, they have still taken up your mandate, be assured that you will never get the required mind-space from them and they may not be able to strike a deal for you. Why do large merchant bankers pick up smaller deals then? Well, the reasons could be many, including the possibility that someone has put in a word and persuaded them to take up your case. In such a case, they cannot be convinced to get you a guaranteed deal. With Prime Securities, our deal was of interest. The deal size would not have been that large, but it seemed important for them to start doing deals in the Internet space and create their references in the sector, which was why they valued our mandate.

- The merchant banker must have good connections. Connections may not seal deals all the time, but they do open doors, allowing you to pitch your case. Having connections also enables the merchant banker to know who is investing in different sectors and to identify the target prospects. It also opens up alternate channels of investment other than the traditional VCs, like the High Net worth Individuals (HNI) or corporate investors. Through Vamesh's contacts, we were able to meet such investors too.

o As you will be spending a lot of time with the merchant banker, it is very important to have a comfort level between the both of you. He will probably know some of your biggest secrets, be it related to a business idea or some weakness in your model. To enable him to do his job the best, you will have to open up to him adequately. For all these to happen, it is necessary to have an excellent chemistry and an extremely comfortable relationship with the merchant banker. In our case, we had both in Vamesh.

These were, in fact, the most compelling factors that made us choose him to raise our funds.

Having chosen Vamesh, we gave our official mandate to Prime Securities. An agreement was signed.

The commercial terms included a "success only" fee, which meant that we would pay them only if we were able to strike a deal and raise the money. The percentage agreed upon was five percent of the deal size. In case they were unsuccessful in getting us the investment, we would pay them nothing and they could consider their efforts waste.

That we could begin work with our first choice merchant banker, and that too, on a "success only" fee made us feel wonderful. If they had asked us for upfront money, in any case, we would have not been able to pay because we did not have any serious cash reserves.

The terms that we were offered were clearly a sign of positivity that reigned in the air during those times. Little did we know then that the trend would reverse soon. But for now, we were in a period just prior to the dotcom boom, where everything looked positive and vibrant in the Internet space, where companies like Prime Securities felt the need to secure some Internet deals and they were willing to go to great lengths to achieve them. We were not complaining!

The mandate was exclusive. Till we were in agreement, which was for 90 days, we were not supposed to engage any other merchant banker to raise funds. In short, Prime Securities had 90 days to get us a deal. If they could not find us the deal, then the exclusivity clause would be waived off and we could work with other merchant bankers. The exclusivity clause, however, did not stop us from talking directly to investors, if we wanted to. And if some investors were talking to us directly and they ended up making an investment, then Prime Securities would stand to get nothing out of the deal. This was a clause that would get relevant in time, as we were to see later.

All in all, the terms of the agreement seemed to be more than fair to us. Such terms were only possible because of the boom time. And that was some boom time. The beginning of the mad rush to the dotcom IPOs (at least in the US). Startups with very less capital were raising huge funds. And if merchant bankers ever demanded an upfront fee, the choice would have been simple for them— get another merchant banker.

Brainstorming for a Business Plan

Having signed the deal, we began brainstorming on the business plan. Vamesh talked to us about the need of a business plan. We knew the fundamental English meaning of the term, but there was just a whole lot to learn beyond that.

We would churn out Excel spreadsheets, have series of meetings with the investors, carefully evaluating their feedback, and then we would be back to the meetings with Vamesh to brainstorm the business plan, all over again.

We knew that we had a potential winner. Our free Online Post service had gone viral and a large number of NRIs were using the service. We also knew that we had revenue opportunities - both in terms of advertising and in selling online gifts to the same NRIs who were using the Online Post service.

We knew this much. Beyond that was pure gut feel.

What would be the size of the market? How would we scale it up? How much money should we raise? If we raised the money at all, would we be able to utilise it to the fullest? When and how will we make the big money? Who were our competitors? The questions never stopped and there were no clear answers in sight.

One of the prime concerns was also the valuation of the company. Considering that we were a fledgling company with little to show,

If I Had To Do It Again…
Enter the VC

in terms of serious revenues or profits, how do we lead the investors to a substantial amount? And if we were to raise the capital, at what value of the company should we allow our equity to be purchased by the investors?

It took several brainstorming sessions with Vamesh and a few others from the Prime Securities team, before we began seeing a semblance of a business plan emerge. However, there was still a lot of speculation. Being the very early days of the Internet in India, the real growth of the medium was a big question.

Would cyber cafes mushroom at every nook and corner and make Online Post service irrelevant? Online Post service had gone viral, but how far will its popularity spread? If we had to scale up our business and make the NRIs, who were using our Online Post service for free, spend money on our site, how do we do that? Not only that, we would like them to increase their spending with time. How do we achieve that? Or would there be enough advertising money to justify running only the free Online Post service? There were no clear answers.

Being an early player in a new industry puts you in this kind of a situation. On one hand, there are no easy references to benchmark upon. You have to set your own benchmarks. That is a negative. On the other hand, nobody else knows better. For example, they may not be sure whether to appreciate a 100 percent growth rate or feel there is still scope for more growth.

Be that as it may, we had a business plan to make. And we had no choice but to let Excel sheet leave its mark as we projected growth rates and created the business plan numbers, essentially on extrapolation methods.

Upping Our Defences

The revenue and growth figures may have been based on assumptions, but we realised that we had to learn to defend our plan when we met the investors. As a result, we began getting grilled in mock sessions at Prime Securities. Slowly, we started getting comfortable with the grilling sessions.

Here is how we defended. We started estimating the NRI population across the world, especially in the US. We then estimated the percentage of them on the Internet and the number of close relations they could have back in India. We also estimated how many of them would want to communicate using a service like Online Post and also be interested in Online Gifting. We then projected the potential market numbers.

But then, how do we reach out to them? What would be our marketing methodologies? Vigorously going viral, advertising, participating in Indian events abroad, what else? We started estimating the number of potential customers that we could acquire through these activities.

But before that, we had to address the logistics challenges.

With the Online Post and Online Gifting services, it was not just bits and bytes that our servers had to take care of. Like mentioned before, it was also lot of physical labour that we all had to put in.

After all, the letters had to be printed on paper, put into envelopes with postage stamps and then mailed out. Whether free or not, we had to take ownership and responsibility of ensuring that the letters reached the recipients fine. With the growth that we were anticipating, we had to devise an extremely robust process for the whole activity.

On the gifting front, things seemed even more complicated. We had to grapple with a whole lot of issues like the variety of products that we would have on the site, their procurement, their packaging and shipment - would we have our suppliers ship on our behalf or should we handle the product shipments ourselves? Will we be able to procure products whenever we needed them or would we have to keep an inventory?

All these questions had to be tackled and we only had assumptions to our aid. These assumptions were more of educated guesses based on informal market research, rather than a proper market research.

After much effort and after confronting questions that we had not even contemplated earlier, we were finally able to put together a business plan. By then, Vamesh had started sending out meeting requests to prospective investors.

Meeting the VCs

In 1998, true-blue VCs were few and several of them were just setting foot into India. Besides them, there was a host of 'wannabe' VCs. As we began our meetings, we chanced to meet a few of every type.

The first gentleman whom Vamesh took us to meet was someone, who he was sure would not invest, but whose interaction would be of utmost value to us. The gentleman was Abhay Havalder, part of the Draper Venture Fund that had invested in Rediff.com and UTV's skyshopping business. In all these deals, Prime Securities had acted as the catalyst.

The meeting with Abhay was enlightening. He was a person with a lot of clarity. He gave us a bunch of home truths, not necessarily to question our model, but to enable us to think harder about many issues.

Post the meeting, we have had a few more interactions with him at events like the IndiaEntrepreneurs Meet (a body mainly comprising of dotcom entrepreneurs, formed around that time), at TiE Meets and other similar places. Each time, Abhay managed to leave a mark on us with his knowledge and insight.

Another true-blue VC that Vamesh introduced us to was Sudhir Sethi of Walden. His style of working was very different. He believed that a VC had to spend a lot of time with potential investee prospects, to really 'know' them. In his quest to knowing them, he would try to understand their business model better.

We had quite a few meetings with Sudhir. Usually, he would appear quite informal, ordering snacks and appearing to be in no hurry whatsoever. Couple of times, he even used our Online Post and Gifting services – may be with a view of getting first-hand knowledge about the services.

He also invited us to a couple of gatherings at his office, where we were introduced to some of his investee companies and other investee prospects like us. The idea was to explore synergies among us.

Sudhir was a relatively senior investor, older to us by a few years, and had had substantial corporate experience with companies like Wipro. During our interactions with him, we picked up many pieces of wisdom. For example, he mentioned once how a startup should have a CEO with the right 'head space,' say, someone who has handled a business of Rs 100 crores. Only a person with that level of experience will be able to think how to take a startup to a Rs 100 crores level. A person who has never handled anything more than Rs 10 crores business will not be able to think beyond a certain limit. He also introduced us to a book called 'Crossing the Chasm.' This book almost became like a definitive guide for us to understand what small budding entrepreneurs should be doing (and not doing.)

All these interactions were interesting and our hopes were getting raised about the possibility of getting an investment from Walden Securities. As he used our services and introduced us to his other investee companies, it seemed like he was in a mood to invest in HomeIndia.com. But ultimately after several meetings, things did not work out and we were left a bit disappointed.

While we were meeting Sudhir, we were also meeting other investors. Some of these meetings went over to two-to-three rounds, but somehow, we were not able to break the ice.

However, we kept the faith.

Desperation Trickles In

Sabeer Bhatia, the hero of Indian entrepreneurs, was on one of his many visits to India and we had a chance to hear him tell his story. He talked about how he had met a number of investors, before one of them decided to invest in his venture.

That kindled an inspiration in us. Despite meeting many investors, making the same pitch over and over again, sometimes improvising ourselves or giving the presentation the desired touch, we were not frustrated.

Vamesh on the other hand, perhaps, felt a little more pressure. Though he did not show it openly, maybe the amount of time he was investing in a success-only-fees client, and that the exclusivity period of three months was coming to an end had had him worried. He decided to explore routes other than just the traditional VC. He set up a meeting with a HNI, a breed that is big, rich, powerful and had the guts and the gumption for venture investments.

The gentleman we met was a young generation member of a family that owned one of the largest shipping companies in India. The meeting turned out to be a little different from others. While there was no doubt about the ability of this gentleman to invest in our venture, the type of questions he asked was very different from the ones that we had encountered from the VCs.

His questions mainly revolved around ROI and revenue channels. The VCs whom we had met till then had a fair idea about the dotcom business models, and hence asked about hits and eyeballs. However, this more-conservative-investor was enquiring about issues that were relevant to traditional business models. There were no easy answers to give him, as our business did not immediately meet the demands of an early ROI. He was obviously not a potential 'venture' capitalist! One more investor struck off the list.

We usually met the investors at their offices. In some cases, they came down to the office of Prime Securities. However, there was this meeting with a VC that we held at an old style café in South Mumbai, the Mocambo Café. Not quite a Starbucks. It was an unusual place to hold a meeting. But we did. Considering it to be a part of the quirky dotcom thing!

The meeting was with Rajesh Jog of eVentures, a firm that was very active in dotcom funding during those days. He gave us a patient hearing and was very excited about the HomeIndia.com story, but he wanted to see a bigger picture. Like HomeIndia.com, were we thinking of creating HomePakistan.com or HomeSriLanka.com or HomeKenya.com? Could we go global? At that time, it did not make sense to us and we were wondering what he was talking about. Looking back now, we wonder if there could have been merit in what he was suggesting.

As time passed by, we started wondering if we were going to strike a deal at all. Were we just dreaming big and wasting our time and energy? After a long chat about this dilemma, we finally agreed to give ourselves an inflexible deadline. By March 31, 1999, if we were unable to raise the capital, we would stop the whole exercise and take a call on our futures, differently.

As the deadline was set, we decided to give our best shot. We got few things going.

First, we communicated our anxiety to Vamesh, but not the timeline. We told him that things had to happen now and we were very tired of running around for meetings, without any concrete results.

The second step was to start talking to some of our contacts to explore the investment opportunities directly. As mentioned earlier, our arrangement with Prime Securities was exclusive only in terms of a merchant banking relationship. Direct investment options were open.

Meanwhile, a concerned Vamesh set up a meeting with his CEO, Jaykumar. Jayks or Jakes as Jaykumar is called, was a man of influence. He was an aggressive leader and had enviable networking capabilities. He worked on producing results as a CEO should, and for that he would leave no stones unturned. This was what he did in our case too, when he figured that there was an urgency creeping into our case now.

He set up a meeting with Kabir Mulchandani of Baron Electronics. Kabir came from the business background of consumer electronics. He had been credited of being a game-changer of sorts with regards to the sale of television sets in the Indian market. An ultimate price warrior, Kabir had broken the barriers of pricing on television sets by selling Akai TVs, which were priced at low rates, and had changed the consumer electronics business forever.

Kabir was younger to us by a few years, but his aggression in business knew no bounds. Jayks and he had a tremendous connect. In a way, they were very similar people. Later, we met Kabir at his office in Opera House a couple of times and over lunch too, which included just the two of us and Kabir. We tried to do this with every investor we met. Perhaps, it was a learning from our earlier interactions with Sudhir, where we realised that we had to know our investors better and what is more, we had to see if we connected with them. To assess that, we often met them informally.

It was clear that Kabir was a driven man and would work hard to turn around his investments into success. We also realised that he was trying to aggressively grow in his business and may not be able to give us sufficient time. The other people we met in his organisation did not impress us at all. In fact, they made us uncomfortable.

While we appreciated Kabir's business sense, his drive and his rapid growth in his own business, something about the way he operated made us wary. Still, with the deadline that we had set for ourselves and the fact that at the moment, he was the only potential investor, we went ahead with the discussions.

We finally arrived at discussing the specifics of the investment. Jayks was completely involved in the discussions and negotiations. Kabir was ready to invest Rs 5 crores, in turn he would want a 50 percent stake in the company.

This was certainly very un-VC-like. To perform well, a true VC would want the promoters to have enough stake so that the promoters remain sufficiently incentivised. As against that, an old school investor would think of the other extreme. Since he is putting in his money, he should own most of the company, such that the promoter / founder is almost reduced to a paid employee. This might have worked well in the old economy but would not make any headway in the new economy.

Kabir's deal had somewhere adopted a middle path between a typical VC proposition and that of an old school investor. Though we were not very happy, we were open to exploring the option.

However, what spoilt the opportunity was when the ownership percentage, from being 50-50, was attempted to be made to 51-49 in the investors favor. We showed our obvious discomfort and conveyed it to Vamesh and Jayks. Jayks came back with a modified proposal - Both, Kabir and we, keep 49 percent each and Prime Securities would keep 2 percent as a compensation of their fees for the deal. His idea was that 49-2-49 should give us a lot of comfort to finalise the deal, as he claimed he was neutral to both the parties.

But we were not sure how this neutrality would pan out in the long run. After all, we were a small fish in the whole game. If the plan moved ahead and we signed up, we knew what we were getting into - a business where we would be the minority partners, where strategic changes could be made by Kabir as and when he deemed fit.

We pondered over it. The business needed us - minority or not. Kabir would not be able to just do away with us, as we were critical to the success of the project. With a few crores in the company, even with a minority stake, we had an opportunity to make something out of the business, which wouldn't be the case if we did not have the venture money. On top of that, we had a deadline looming large. We considered accepting the deal.

As the deal with Kabir was progressing, another development was slowly hatching.

When we were reaching out to our contacts, we had got in touch with a powerful IT head of one of India's largest private sector companies. We had connected with him on account of our Internet seminars. He was even the guest speaker for two of our Annual Internet Summits.

He belonged to a large and very ambitious group, which did not have any direct investments in the Internet or even the IT space, but was keen to get there. It was only later that we realised that this gentleman, besides being the IT head of this large group, was also very close to the top echelons of the company, far more than what his designation would require him to be.

We reached out to him. He knew us as respectable Internet entrepreneurs, thanks to the Internet seminars that he had seen us organise. He asked for our presentation. This led to a personal meeting with him, where he had a lot of general questions, about our business, our future plans, about Online Post, about the two of us, our ambitions, and other personal matters. It was a long and interesting interaction and we again began hoping that something would emerge out of this.

We waited for things to move. A few days passed by but we did not hear from him. As our deadline was approaching and even as the Kabir Mulchandani deal was moving ahead, we were desperate to have an alternate option. We followed up with the IT gentleman. After a couple of phone calls where he was giving evasive responses, he finally confirmed that he had set up a 'high-level' meeting. This was to be with a person who was second-in-command of this large group. And the meeting was to take place at around 9:30 pm at their office. Very unusual, but we played along.

The meeting started even later. The IT head gave a brief introduction to the senior leader, who was chairing the meeting. It appeared that this must have been the shortest brief ever given to a senior person about us. It also appeared that it did not matter. After asking us few trivial questions, this senior gentleman began talking about the ambitions of the group, how aggressive they were and how they 'made things happen' in whatever fields they entered. It appeared like an aggressive 'selling' of their idea to us, and not the other way around. They were trying to convince us about the benefits we would reap if we got into an alliance with them. The IT head and four others with him remained silent throughout. It was only at the end that they started talking about the IT plans of the company and their Internet initiatives. Though the discussion was supposed to be in reference to our presence there, it appeared to be a routine internal discussion on their IT / Internet strategy, and we 'just happened to be around!'

Towards the end of the meeting, some specific questions were addressed. However, most of the talking kept happening between the IT head and the senior leader, and we were just interjecting a word here and there.

Soon the discussions veered to details like - where would we be based? Where would our office be? They spoke about letting out a

 If I Had To Do It Again…
Enter the VC

space in their office for us. They even went to an extent of saying that we could potentially get started the next day. By then, the time was 11:30 pm. And they talked about 'the next day start!'

At this point, we managed to put in a small word - that due to various existing commitments, we would not be able to start the next day, but we will get in touch with the IT head to work out more specific details.

Finally, the meeting ended. We exited their office in a daze. Did we actually go through what we went through? Was this how large corporations worked? It was a first for us. One long meeting and supposedly, everything was final. Of course, for us, nothing was final, except for the fact that if we wanted, we could get started with them as early as the next day.

But in what capacity? As promoters, with them coming in as investors? As employees, who were allowed to keep a small share of the company? Or simply as employees? Nothing was clear.

If they were acquiring us, at what value was the deal happening. If they were merging us with them, were we going to get equity in the corporation? Were we getting VC investment from them? Not a clue.

Let's for an instance assume that we joined them, then what were we supposed to do? Were they going to run our business plan or were we supposed to run some other plan that they had? Were they contemplating on taking in only both of us or the entire HomeIndia team to manage the new initiatives? Completely blank on that. We could sense that this corporate group was very ambitious in terms of what they wanted to do in the online space. We could also sense that decision making at their end would be very quick. We could see that investing money was not an issue for them. We could also see that in that one meeting, they had built a respect for both of us. However, what was the business plan that they would want us to deliver on? What would be our roles (entrepreneurs or employees with some stock-options)? What level of delegation would we have in decision making? All these were quite unclear.

But, we knew that we could start on this opportunity the very next day. So a deal was on the table, but we were unsure about the terms.

We were running against the clock on our set deadline and we had two options in front of us. However we were not completely comfortable with either of them. It almost seemed like a choice between the frying pan and the fire. Not exactly the kind of scenario that we had in mind, when we set out to raise funds with Vamesh.

Considering the looming deadline and months of hard work, which had gone in meeting investors to realise our dream of making HomeIndia.com a big brand and a large business, there was no turning back. Now was not the time to consider going back to doing Internet seminars or building corporate websites. We had to make a choice. We had to choose between the two!

We were waiting for a final term sheet from Kabir. A draft had already been seen by us and we had asked Vamesh to get a few clauses amended. At the same time, we had bought some time for ourselves from the corporate, but if we wanted to go with them, we had to get back to them soon before they forgot about us.

 | If I Had To Do It Again…
Enter the VC

Springing Up of a Brilliant Option

As we are grappling to reach a decision on this dilemma, we decided to consult a good friend of Sanjay's - Sandeep Shah, who was a Chartered Accountant. He was highly knowledgeable and we thought it would be worthwhile to take his opinion on both the deals — to understand which one made better sense and the factors that we should be wary of, if we walked into either of the deals.

Sanjay and Sandeep were both fellow Rotarians. When we were doing Internet seminars, Sandeep had once invited Sanjay to share some thoughts about the Internet with his team at his office. It was here that Sanjay had chanced to meet one of Sandeep's elder brothers, Jayendra Shah, who was also a CA. Jayendra appeared to be the most knowledgeable about the new technologies in their team.

Sandeep, Jayendra and their elder brother, Ashok Shah, were all CAs. Together, they had been running a very successful CA firm - N. A. Shah and Associates. They were renowned for their high level of integrity, hard work and sincerity. They had clients who had been with them for many, many years and who trusted them completely. Over the period that we have known them and their business, which is quite some years, we have seen them grow from strength to strength.

Now when we went to meet Sandeep to take his advice on the two deals, he listened to us intently and started taking notes. He then asked a few more questions and went to check if Jayendra was in office. Finding him in office, he quickly arranged a meeting between us. We realised it was to take an additional opinion.

Jayendra, or rather Jayendrabhai, as we referred to him, quickly understood the situation. He validated some of the points that Sandeep had already conveyed to us. Then he took the conversation to a different direction altogether.

He saw that while Kabir was willing to put in Rs 5 crores, he was staking claim to close to half of the company. Jayendrabhai knew we were not comfortable with it.

He then asked a pointed question, "What is the minimum amount of money required to take the company to the next level? Would Rs 2.5 crores work? If yes, then can we settle for 2.5 crores with Kabir and give away only 25 percent of the company?"

This was a new thought. Throughout, we had been working with Rs 5 crores in mind. All our plans and projections were based on that amount. For a moment, we hesitated.

Seeing that, Jayendrabhai clarified that he was suggesting this option because if we really did not require Rs 5 crores at the moment, we could raise Rs 2.5 crores, retain a bigger share in the company, build the company to a certain level and then raise the money once again. This way, we will be able to retain a larger share of the company, even after multiple investment rounds.

We seriously pondered over it. We actually did not have a plan to spend the Rs 5 crores right away, so the opportunity to retain a

| If I Had To Do It Again…
Enter the VC

bigger share in the company suddenly seemed very attractive. We confirmed that this could be quite acceptable.

In fact, even as we had made the business plan, met the investors and talked big numbers, it was still a dream to achieve them. Currently, we were doing only a small business worth a few lakhs, not even a crore and we were talking about raising Rs 5 crores. Almost surreal!

We also admitted that since the investment was soon to become a reality, there was an anxiety of sorts. Also the questions – do we actually require so much cash? What do we really want this money for? What were we going to do with it?

Being a dotcom business, there were ample opportunities for advertising. We could easily blow up Rs 5 crores on advertising and other promotions. If Rs 5 crores could buy advertisements, then so could Rs. 2.5 crores. In short, the whole situation was quite unreal and it was not so difficult to confirm that raising Rs 2.5 crores and having a bigger share in the company would give us greater comfort.

Jayendrabhai was looking at us, and we were wondering if Kabir would agree to this proposal of putting in lesser money and owning lesser share in the company. Quite unlikely. We knew he would not settle for anything less than the 49 percent that we had agreed upon.

That was when Jayendrabahi dropped a bomb. Now that Rs 2.5 crore seemed a decent amount to raise, could we look at some of his clients who may be interested in investing in our company? We looked at him, quite unable to believe what we were hearing. Yet another option was opening up, and a far better one than what we currently had. This sounded too good to be true, yet we knew the constraints involved. For such deals to close, it would take a long time. For us, it would mean meeting investors once again and we, of course, could not ignore the impending deadline. We conveyed our concerns to Jayendrabahi and he calmly said he could close the deal in three to four days.

As mentioned earlier, N. A. Shah and Associates is an eminent Chartered Accountancy firm. This we knew, but what we did not know was that they also facilitated and invested in ventures. In fact, if we had known this, we might have formally pitched to them like we had done with many other VCs. Not that Jayendrabhai or N. A. Shah had done a large number of investments, but they had done a few. And now, as our case had come up before them, they were giving it a serious thought.

We believe there were a few clear-cut reasons why Jayendrabhai would have thought of HomeIndia as a worthwhile investment:

- o Both of us came from a business background. Thus, we would like to believe that Jayendrabhai believed we knew the "value" of money.

- o A dotcom plan which was 'the' place to invest those days. Maybe it was still early days in India, but Jayendrabhai prided himself of being well-read about international matters and knowing what global trends were. HomeIndia.com then seemed like an apt opportunity to get an early foot into tomorrow's winning sector.

 | If I Had To Do It Again…
Enter the VC

- A business plan that had been validated by other investors, who were on the verge of investing. Now, that was a big positive.

No wonder his mind worked overtime to try and facilitate an alternate deal for us.

We asked Jayendrabhai to work on raising the money for us within four days, as promised. Sure enough, in four-days, Jayendrabhai called to confirm that he already had a commitment to the tune of Rs 1.5 crores. Another Rs 50 lakhs was on its way and he was awaiting the final confirmation. This was enough for us to confirm our interest in this deal and move to the next step.

The next step was for Jayendrabhai to create (and for us to validate and accept) the draft of the shareholder's agreement that would govern the deal. In normal cases of investment, this stage would have taken a while. However, in this case, with a timeline on our heads, everything moved rapidly. Jayendrabhai already had a few ready draft agreements to pick from. After a few changes that we suggested, the draft was cleared. That was one tick on the list.

Next came the due-diligence. Due diligence is a process wherein the factual data shared by both the companies are verified. Again, this process could have been a lengthy one. As we were racing against time and were a small company, there was nothing much to check. The due diligence process was planned and completed in exactly one day, in fact, in a few hours. Jayendrabhai and his team of CAs came over and checked our books of accounts and our processes. That was it. Due-diligence was done, and we were all set then to move to the final step. The signing of the shareholder's agreements and getting in the cheques.

Although the decision was final and everything was under control, Jayendrabhai required few more days to organise the cheques from his investors.

Taking into consideration the time it would take for the cheques to come in, we decided upon the signing date as March 23, 1999. Now that was a sheer coincidence. Because, it was exactly three years ago - March 23, 1996 that we had launched our first business venture, where we had conducted our first ever Internet seminar at Hotel Atithi in Santa Cruz. And it was exactly a year back on March 23, 1998 that our private limited company was incorporated. We smiled at the coincidence. March 23 was indeed an auspicious date and we were glad that we were singing the deal on that date. We were also happy that we had adhered to the deadline we had set for ourselves and were able to close a deal before the due date.

Now that everything was sorted, we diverted our attention to an important matter that had been left unaddressed. Communicating this development and our final decision to Vamesh. He had worked hard with us and although a true blue VC deal could not get accomplished, he had managed to bring Kabir on the table to invest in our venture. But then for us, our business and our careers were far more critical, and truly, the deal that we were getting into with Jayendrabhai Shah was far superior in quality than the one that we could have signed with Kabir. So the choice had been an easy one. But this had to be conveyed to Vamesh.

Only once the deal with Jayendrabhai was finalised and frozen, could we close the door on the deal with Kabir. Because we had seen enough to know that a deal could slip through even at the last minute.

We waited till March 22 - a day before we were to sign the deal with Jayendrabhai to convey the fait accompli to Vamesh. We met and told him about all that had transpired. It was not a comfortable situation as we had developed an emotional bond with him. He questioned us a lot but ultimately realised that we had rejected his deal over the new one.

Tough as it was, we were relieved that it was behind us.

But it was not quite that way. Vamesh called us again and said that Jayks wanted to meet us once. We knew that Jayks was a persuasive person and it would not be easy to talk him out. We tried to see if we could avoid the meeting by suggesting how busy we were. Vamesh asked how much time we had before we signed. And we replied that it was just one day. That indeed was the fact. But he wanted us to meet Jayks anyway. Ultimately, we figured out that we could not deny them the meeting. After all, we had been working with them for many months and they deserved this meeting.

But really, there was very little time on hand.

So, where we had the agreement signing scheduled for 10:30 am at the Nariman Point office of N. A. Shah and Associates, we lined up a breakfast meeting with Jayks and Vamesh at the Oberoi for 9 am.

At the meeting, they tried to enquire why we were backing out of the deal and what were the issues, and if there was any scope for renegotiations. It was a last ditch effort on the part of Prime Securities to hold on to the deal. However, we were quite clear that we would lend them a patient hearing but there would be no change in our decision. So politely, we conveyed our final regret and bid them goodbye.

We walked out of Hotel Oberoi Towers and made our way to N. A. Shah office in Mittal Chambers, C-Wing. One of the biggest moments of our lives was waiting for us.

First Round of Investment Becomes a Reality

At the office, almost everything was in order. We went through the elaborate shareholder's agreement one more time. Though all the investors were not present, we were to sign it then. Later, we were to get a copy of the agreement, while the originals were to be left behind to be circulated amongst the various investors for their signatures.

The shareholder's agreement essentially spelt out several clauses. Like the fact that we could not take any major decisions without the investors' clearances, even though they were minority shareholders. Major decisions would include, for example, purchase of large assets, changes in equity structure, and the like. It also spelt out that we would need to go in for Initial Public Offering (IPO) in three to five years. In case we were unable to, then the investors could find other ways to divest their equity. And a variety of other such technical but critical clauses. However, none that worried us. It was clear that daily operations would pretty much be in our hands and we would not have to take permissions from the investors or their representatives for the same. Yes, there would be a Director on the Board, representing the investors and that would be Jayendrabhai. We were quite comfortable with this choice. It was clear that it would only be Jayendrabhai who would represent all the investors and we will not have to go to all of them each time we needed something from them.

After this, we had to sort out the bank accounts in which the invested amount would be deposited. It was decided that the larger amount would be put in an escrow account, where one of the signatories would be Jayendrabhai and the

other would be either one of us. Apart from this, there would be another regular operating account where Jayendrabhai's signature would not be required. This was how it would function. We would periodically present our plans and the required budgets. The amount would then be transferred from the joint account to the regular operational current account. That way, Jayendrabhai could track the broad utilisation of funds and we did not have to go to him for every routine operational requirement. That seemed like a good arrangement.

We used this system quite effectively. We would take proper account statements and get cheques signed from Jayendrabhai. The money would then be transferred to our operational account. Over time, a trust was established between us such that the system was done away with and we were operating both the accounts independently. This was also necessary because Jayendrabhai had to travel a lot, and sometimes this caused minor delays in managing our cash requirements. Although the system provided options in such a case, in terms of Sandeep Shah being an official alternate director and alternate signatory for cheques, it was an arrangement that we rarely used. So over time, we found that it was easier to do away with the joint signing of cheques and managing the bank accounts on our own.

Coming back to the signing of the agreement, there were many copies of the agreement to be signed (one for each investor and there were several investors coming on board). After we finished signing, the cheques were handed over to us. Now the only thing that remained was to transfer the shares in the names of various investors in the coming few days.

Phew! Finally, we had raised our first round of investment - Rs 2.5 crores. Though all the cheques were not in, we did have cheques worth about Rs 1.5 crores. The deal was sealed, the money was in. Our fledgling business worth a few lakhs of rupees had been valued at Rs 10 crores, allowing us to raise this investment. It seemed like a dream. Unbelievable. No collateral given, no sureties. And the money was in.

Our parents and families could not believe it. They all came from traditional businesses (well, we did too). And this was as unreal as it could get. VC was an absolutely new phenomenon for India. And while you still read about these in the papers, that it could happen to you was incredible.

We let it sink in. Having started the day with breakfast at the Oberoi, we allowed ourselves the indulgence of going to the Taj for lunch, and not start worrying, just yet, about how our life was going to change from that point. That was kept for the later!

The money that we raised was not a traditional VC. It was more of an Angel Investment, as it is called. An investment essentially by HNIs – a banker from the UK, a pharma company head honcho, a diamond merchant and few other minor investors. We were apparently going the very traditional way of startups – first round from angels, second from the VCs, then maybe from Private Equity investors, before we hit the IPO. Well, at least that was the dream. We were on the first rung of the long ladder. The journey had just begun.

The Wisdom Nugget

➤ It is generally said that "the colour of money is the same, irrespective of who is giving the money." This is completely un-true. While choosing an investor (whether a HNI or a VC or any other kind of investor), meeting of heart and mind is more important than agreement upon numbers.

➤ Just as an investor would do due-diligence on your business (and your antecedents), you must also conduct a similar due-diligence. Spend lot of time with your prospective financial partner (outside the negotiation room) and try to understand their value system and the way they think.

➤ Every investor will be very happy if things work out well for the business. But try to visualise how the investor would behave if things did not work well…will he pull the plug in a hurry…or be there to support you like a partner?

Chapter 5
A US Office, M&A Offers

Living a Dream, Holding Out for More!

Here we were, having raised the first round of angel money.

Even as the money came into the bank - cheques with lot of zeroes at the end, numbers that we had not seen before - we felt incredulous. We would often wonder what it was that we had done to deserve all this. But again, that was a part of the process we were in, a journey that was just happening.

The whole aspect of angel investment and venture capital fell in place beautifully. The idea that somebody was willing to invest that kind of money, largely betting on the two of us, hoping and expecting us to create something interesting, something of a lot more value, was overwhelming and at the same time humbling. We decided to grab the opportunity and make the most of it.

Putting into Action the Business Plan

As part of our business plan, one of the steps we had proposed was to move closer to our customers. Our customers – the NRIs spread across the globe, who were using our services via the Internet and paying for it too. So far, we connected with them only through emails or via our website. We had to do more. We had to understand them better, go closer to them and market ourselves in their geographies. This was how we could enhance and grow our business further. We soon started working on that strategy.

First of all, we got a new office space. Before we got the investment, we were working out of two separate offices, a small space in Sanjay's office at Dadar and another at Tardeo. The team, split into two, sat in each of the two small offices. It was an interesting arrangement, very typical of bootstrapped startups.

Now that we had the money, one of the objectives was to consolidate both the offices into one. After scouting a bit, we found an interesting space in Lower Parel, just opposite the Phoenix Mills. We got the place done up in some style, though not very extravagant. After all, it had to look like an office of an interesting Internet business. Boy! Was it exciting to move into a furnished office!

The next step was to focus on hiring a few key people. We had two critical positions to be filled - first a person for advertising sales, which was the key revenue generator for Online Post service. Second, a person with a strong logistics background to set up a foolproof workflow and to manage effectively the delivery of letters and gifts, received through Online Post service. We also wanted robust processes in place so as to ensure 100 percent delivery, with no room for error.

Hiring at such senior levels was a first time experience for us. We decided to involve our investor and Director Jayendrabhai Shah to do a round of interviews with the people we had shortlisted. In the end, with everyone's combined efforts, we did manage to find three great resources for the critical positions open with us.

Team in place

For the logistics role, we appointed Deepankar Sen, who was holding a senior operations position in a multinational company. To ensure the website had quality content, we hired a fairly senior journalist, Ramprasad Sahu. To lead advertising sales, Harmeet Singh Arora was brought in.

Along with the three key people, we also hired a few designers, software developers and some support staff for the operations team. Now, we had the complete team ready.

Beyond the new office and the hiring of the team, we were still not spending the money that we had with us. One day, one of the investors walked in to see how we were doing. He was happy with what he saw - that we had a new office teeming with an enthusiastic team. However, he was concerned that we were yet not into big-time marketing. After all, the growth that we needed to bring in quickly was not going to come through a new office or new hires. We had to spend the marketing money. We realised that we had to come out of our 'small-business' approach, and really push the pedal hard on our marketing efforts.

For the first time, we went around looking for an advertising and Public Relation agency. No sooner had we sent the brief out, that we had a stream of people pitching to us, some even very senior. We

If I Had To Do It Again…
Living a Dream, Holding Out for More!

were amazed. We were not a big account like a Coke or a Pepsi and did not have crores of rupees to spend on advertising, yet people were interested in us. That was the flavor of the dotcom weaving its magic. Everybody wanted to ride the dotcom wave, hence big agencies were willing to come and pitch to us because they wanted their share of the dotcom pie.

Another interesting phenomenon was that there were companies who were willing to offer us their services in return of equity in our company. As stories of huge valuations of dotcom businesses in the US were doing rounds, they also wanted a share in the dotcom business. We could possibly get services, without paying any cash, as long as we were willing to give some equity instead. That was the kind of madness that prevailed at that time – a bubble that everyone was riding. Neither did they see anything wrong, nor did we.

We were tempted to give away shares, but reckoned that if the agencies were willing to take our shares instead of lakhs of rupees, our shares were obviously very valuable. We decided not to give our shares. We were clear that we would pay only cash, and not give out any equity.

We finally appointed an advertising agency. As a startup, it was an interesting exercise that we went through, in deciding which agency to choose. What really appealed to us was that the advertising agency we hired exhibited a personal touch. In the team was a key person, who was very creative and exuded a huge amount of enthusiasm, and he was willing to handle our account. We immediately concurred that this was the person we should work with. Aside from the ideas, he seemed to share the same passion that we had, for our business. The bigger agencies had big clients, so we were unsure of their involvement - they might just put some juniors to service our account. Hence, we zeroed down on a mid-sized advertising agency, with an extremely passionate person to handle our account.

The agency was called Dart Advertising and the key person was Naren Belliapa. Over time, they became an important partner for us. They helped create a new logo for HomeIndia.com. They came up with stationery designs and also designs for our packaging materials, which were used to ship the e-commerce orders. And of course, they created some out-of-the-box print advertisements, which went into international editions of India Today, Stardust, and even into several Indian newspapers in the US, and other kinds of magazines and newspapers, which were popular among the NRIs. Most of the advertisements were full-page-coloured ones, while a few were black and white, and others were strips in newspapers and magazines. As time went by, we did a lot of experiments with our print advertising.

We also decided to create a Television Commercial (TVC) for Indian TV channels in North America. While Dart was involved in the storyboarding and scripting of the TVC, we needed someone to actually make the commercial for us. This called for a production house. Dart introduced us to a couple of TVC makers. Finally, we ended up selecting a very reputed filmmaker, Kailash Surendranath. He created our first TV advertisement, which was an experience in itself. It was fascinating to watch the gamut of motions of shooting, editing and viewing the final cuts, before the advertisement went on air.

 If I Had To Do It Again...
Living a Dream, Holding Out for More!

Next, we had to find the TV channels where we could air our advertisement. There were Indian TV programmes being telecasted in the US. Interestingly, they were mainly shows and episodes already broadcasted in India. Today, a satellite channel beams programmes all over the world. However, during those times, things were different. Apart from the Indian TV programmes, there were some local Indian channels catering to NRIs such as Namaste Asia. We hunted for all such popular channels and booked our slots. We finally ran our advertisement, and our marketing activity started taking shape in the true sense.

All these developments were happening while we were still in India. In our business plan, we had specified that as soon as we raised the investment, we would build our presence in the US. We were to meet the NRIs, attend various events and functions and talk to them. We also had to connect with brands and companies, who had access to a large number of NRIs and explore if alliances could be struck. We wanted to be close to our market to seek opportunities, which could ensure our rapid growth. With that in mind, we made plans to build our presence in the US.

Initially, both of us made short visits to the US - once in 30 to 60 days, where we attended a few events, met some people and came back. Then, we decided that one of us would stay back in the US for a longer duration and actually set up an office there. We soon completed all the paperwork related to the US office, which was a slightly tedious process. The plan was to start the US office as early as 2000. Between us, we decided that I would manage the India operations, while Sanjay would set up the US operations. Sanjay would go to the US and be there for four to five months and set it up. By the time it was summer, his children would have finished their term in school, and then his family could join him. On that note, it was decided that Sanjay would move to the US by early 2000.

An Interesting Development

Meanwhile, when all this planning was going on, an interesting development was happening alongside. Few months after we had got the investment, someone from Citibank came to meet us. He was an intermediary, representing a large US based company and was supposedly exploring an interest that the company showed in us. We were not very sure about their actual intention then. But gradually, realised that they were looking at us from an acquisition point of view. The US company, apparently, was on lookout to acquire some Indian companies in the dotcom space and they were thinking about us.

It was in March 1999 that we got the angel investment, and this development was happening in August 1999. Unbelievable, we thought!

The US company was Mail.com Inc. The reason for their interest in India was that they owned a long list of domain names and one of them was India.com. During that heightened space of large valuations of dotcoms, their intention was to acquire Indian dotcoms and aggregate them on a single platform, and create a massive property under India.com.

 If I Had To Do It Again…
Living a Dream, Holding Out for More!

Soon, a person from Mail.com came down from the US to meet us. We had extensive rounds of discussions over the next few days. Everything went on a positive note and they looked keen to acquire us. They now wanted us to visit New York and meet the owner and senior members of the company to discuss the valuations. We decided to go in December. Everything was happening very fast. In March 1999, we raised the capital and by December, we were supposed to go to Wall Street, New York to discuss the value of an acquisition!

New York, Here We Come for Valuation

Amid cold December winters, we, along with Jayendrabhai, left for New York to meet the key people at Mail.com. The journey is still etched fresh in our memories. The day that we were flying in to New York, there was a heavy storm. As we flew from London, almost all the flights except for ours and one or two others, were cancelled due to the weather conditions. As the plane landed in JFK

Airport, New York, all we could see all around was heavy snow. The white blanket of snow looked exciting, as if beckoning us to a world of possibilities… the forthcoming meetings, the possibility of a big upside…everything actually

seemed exhilarating.

The Mail.com office was in the heart of Manhattan, close to the Wall Street. In fact, close to the iconic statue of the 'bull' there. Just being there for this meeting was a magical feeling and we felt we were close to sealing a deal worth a lot of money.

On the first day, we met the senior team at Mail.com and gave them an overview of what we did, the nature of our business, and the numbers. While everything looked good, our numbers failed to impress them. However, they could see the enterprise and found what we were doing as fascinating. The Online Post service, especially, was a big hit. There was no one else who was doing anything similar.

The US market valued dotcoms on basis of the 'eyeballs' or the user traffic that they were drawing. On account of the fundamental limited user base at that time, Indian dotcoms had not reached those millions of eyeballs level yet. The US market was used to a large market and big numbers, and India was comparatively very small then. They understood this, and considering their plans to build India.com, their interest in us continued, but they had concerns around the valuations.

The second day was spent in intense negotiations. We briefly met the owner of Mail.com. He was an extremely busy man and we had a very brief meeting, wherein he asked pointed, probing questions about numbers and growth. As he was in the process of acquiring us, it was only fair that he asked those questions.

After this meeting, the Mail.com team was supposed to deliberate internally. At our end, we reckoned that we would need the help of a local legal expert, and since we had the day to ourselves, we decided to meet one. We got through the lawyer via some reference. He was supposedly a very busy man and since we were approaching him at such a short notice, the only time-slot he could give was us lunch hour. We joined him for lunch. We still remember that afternoon vividly. The lawyer was courteous enough to host us lunch and the

If I Had To Do It Again…
Living a Dream, Holding Out for More!

meeting continued for an hour, where we discussed our points. However, this turned out to be the most expensive luncheon we had ever had. Every minute that he spent with us was billable, which we got to know when his bill came and we had to pay it. Yes, a very expensive lunch indeed.

The next day, we went to meet our key contact point at Mail.com- the same person who had travelled to India. He was our single point of contact for the acquisition discussions at Mail.com. We sat across the table to negotiate the deal and decide the valuation. Since, we had recently raised the investment, we were in no hurry to sell. Hence, we were trying to negotiate the best deal. Another point was that, Mail.com was not intending to give us cash, but a share of their equity that was listed on the NASDAQ. The listed shares were treated as liquid currency, but the restriction was that there was a lock-in period and we could not sell the shares for a few years.

All this sounded fine, conceptually. However, the Mail.com stock was an unknown area to us. We had no idea if the current price was indeed a fair price, or how the stock was going to perform in the future. Also, irrespective of how we performed in the next few years when we were locked-in, we would still not be able to seriously influence the stock. For us, it was a gamble in terms of the future valuations of the Mail.com stock. It was our entire life's hard work at stake, while for them, it was simply another acquisition. Our stakes were definitely higher than theirs.

Another concern we had was the huge hole that Indian Income Tax department would burn in our pockets. Even if Mail.com gave us the stocks, we still would have to pay capital gains tax, on the basis of the entire value. We would be in a situation, where we would get equity, which was locked-in, and hence not liquid, and still have to pay crores from our pocket as tax, as if we had got the entire amount in liquid cash. That was indeed a huge burden.

Understanding all these factors, we were trying to negotiate hard to get some decent money in cash, while for the rest of the amount, we were willing to accept the shares.

After tough negotiations, we finally reached some kind of conclusion. We tabled the minutes of the meeting and agreed upon it. Looked like we had finally pulled through a decent deal. We celebrated over dinner and wine, and enjoyed the moment.

We felt great and soon concluded our short visit to New York and returned to India. We felt like we had clinched a fantastic deal.

Turn of Events

Once in India, we continued with our business and waited for the detailed paperwork, which Mail.com team was supposed to dispatch to us. We were not celebrating till the big money found its way into our bank. Then one afternoon, we got a call from our point of contact at Mail.com, the same person, who had initially come to visit us. He spoke slowly, in a low voice, "Our boss is still not comfortable with the valuation." We listened.

We were valued at Rs 70 crores (USD 17 million.) This was almost a 700 percent jump from our earlier valuation of Rs 10 crores. There

 | If I Had To Do It Again…
Living a Dream, Holding Out for More!

was something very unreal about it, hence they were not convinced and were not willing to seal the deal. They were, however, open to re-negotiations.

But we were not.

After all, they had gone back on their word. We felt they were being unfair. After having hammered out the deal in New York, if we were asked to go back to the negotiation table, then this was not the company we wanted to go back to. We walked out of the deal.

As mentioned, a large part of the deal money was going to come to us in the form of stocks. Later, we were to find out that when the dotcom crash happened, the Mail.com stock took a huge beating. From USD 10, it went down to a few cents and after some time, it exited out of the Exchange. In case, we had gone ahead with the deal, we would have been left with nothing. In a way, it was a blessing in disguise that the deal failed.

Getting Back to Business

Putting the entire episode behind us and going by our original plan, Sanjay went back to the US in early 2000 to set up our office. Northern California in the Silicon Valley was chosen to be our base. Sanjay spent about three to four months there. Although he had been a student in the US, way back in 1985-86, these three to four months were a new learning for him. In fact, it was kind of a relearning - from finding an apartment, to taking up a car on rent and learning to drive there, to moving around to different cities in the US on his own, without any support, even while focusing on

the purpose he was there for - building the US office of Homeindia.
com.

Early 2000 – the boom time in the Silicon Valley. Apartments were
hard to find and the rents were exceptionally high. It was the dotcom
boom days and everybody was apparently making a lot of money.
Having said that, it was exciting to be there - to meet a lot of people
and feel the boom seep in.

Another Interesting Development

Around that time, another interesting development started taking
shape. While the Mail.com story was a thing of past, Valucom, based
in Chicago, began showing interest in us. Valucom sold calling
cards - meaning using their cards, one could call India from within
the US, at low rates. It was a very popular service among the NRIs
and aligned well with our Online Post and Online Gifting services.
Both were reaching out to the same target audience. We had already
done some transactional barter deals with Valucom and had a good
working relationship in place. Now, a meeting was set up to explore
what more we could do. Sanjay was looking at it as an opportunity
to do more business, so he went to Chicago and spent a day with
them at their office. Two extremely smart businessmen, both of
Indian origin - Arvind Singh and Sandeep Srivastava - ran Valucom.
The meeting went off exceptionally well and by the end of the day,
we were exploring the idea of possibly merging our businesses to
make it a much bigger whole. We realised there was great synergy
between both the companies.

 If I Had To Do It Again…
Living a Dream, Holding Out for More!

Valucom was already at a certain level, doing a business to the tune of USD 10 million. We were still growing. In such a scenario, the idea of a joint venture or a strong partnership or a merger with Valucom indeed seemed very interesting and something that would create a win-win situation for both our businesses.

Shortly thereafter, Sanjay returned to India. And we further debated on the proposition. We interacted with Arvind and Sandeep over emails and continued to exchange ideas. We were more convinced than ever that there was a great ground to work on. With that thought in mind, both Arvind and Sandeep came down to India to meet us. We spent a couple of days thrashing things out, interacting and understanding the opportunity.

They were two Indian entrepreneurs and we were two Indian entrepreneurs, somewhat similar in age, we thought alike, we were excited and passionate, and here was an amazing opportunity to work together. We had a conceptual understanding about the valuation because we all knew that it would be a merger and not an acquisition. We would fundamentally swap shares at an agreed-upon ratio, form a common company and work as a single unit.

The next step before inking the deal was to conduct a due diligence on both the companies. We had to verify each others' books of accounts and ensure that everything was in place. Valucom found a well-known Indian company to audit us. At our end, we decided that since Sanjay had already seen their establishment in Chicago, it would be apt for me and Jayendrabhai to visit their office and also undertake the due diligence process. We decided to hire an auditor in the US who could carry out the due diligence on

Valucom. We got them on board to join me and Jayendrabhai at Chicago. Simultaneously, Valucom sent a person to India to check our accounts, while Sanjay held the fort.

Soon, the mutual due diligence was completed. However, Jayendrabhai and I returned to India with some skepticism. During the due diligence, we observed that the Valucom business was currently operating on diminishing returns. This perhaps, might have been one of the reasons why they were keen to get into a joint venture with us.

In such a scenario, aligning with them on the share agreement ratio that was initially decided upon, did not seem very attractive. The share swap ratio was based on the revenue ratio. As they had higher revenues, they were to get a larger share of the equity swap. However, we now felt that we were growing better and faster, while they were treading on a negative path. From that point, the ratio did not seem justified. And it was just about a year since we had raised our investment. Did we have to hurry and get into a deal that we were not comfortable with? Did we not have several options to grow our business and get bigger and better valuations? Yes, we did. On that note, we decided to walk out of the deal.

In a span of just one year, two potential deals fell into our laps, but neither materialised. One deal, where we walked out and another deal, where the other party walked out. Not bad to begin with. We had deals coming our way, an office in the US and a robust business plan that focused on scaling up our growth. We decided to focus on growing our business and were certain that money would follow. What we were ignorant about, at that point of time, was the

 | If I Had To Do It Again…
Living a Dream, Holding Out for More!

vulnerability of the dotcom bubble – a bubble that was on the verge of bursting.

Had we known, would we have taken a different call? We don't know. We had not foreseen to that extent. At that moment, we were extremely positive about our business and hoped to take it to great heights. Knowing this, we walked out of both the deals.

Looking back, did we do things right? Just to tell you the story of Valucom. A few months after we had walked out of the deal, Rediff acquired them. Rediff was already listed on NASDAQ and Valucom got a good valuation. Following which, both Arvind and Sandeep exited the company in some time.

Had we done the deal with Valucom, would Rediff have acquired that merged venture? Would we have got a better valuation? We could have. Did we know this development would have taken place? No, we did not. Could it have happened in some other way? It could have. In the hindsight, everything looks fine. Did we repent even for a moment? No, we did not. It was destiny that brought us to that point, and it was again destiny that did not allow us to proceed

further from that point. In turn, we ended up doing other exciting things to develop our business.

The Wisdom Nugget

➤ Once an investor puts money into your business, he expects you to start putting it to good use immediately. He is not interested in seeing the money lying in your bank. He is clearly looking at the entrepreneur leveraging the capital to create more value at a fast pace.

➤ As an entrepreneur, it is unlikely that you will have expertise in every aspect of running a business. Look at hiring people smarter than you. If you are the smartest guy in the company, then the growth of the company is limited to the extent of your own abilities only.

➤ When you are engaging external vendors, locate people who will find value in the business that you are giving them. If you engage large vendors, you will end up becoming a 'small' customer for them. Our desire to have Dart as our advertising agency was taken with this perspective and we felt we always had access to their top management, as and when we needed it.

➤ In fast growing business like the digital space, there will be a constant stream of new opportunities coming your way. These could be new business ideas or revenue streams, or opportunities to join hands with other companies. Evaluate such opportunities for their worth, even pursue those that appear interesting, but ensure that you do not take your eyes off the ball, viz. your core business focus!

 If I Had To Do It Again…
Living a Dream, Holding Out for More!

Chapter 6

The Dot-com Bust

End of a Fantasy, Back to Reality

Sanjay continued his stay in India. While the deal with Valucom did not come through, few other developments were taking place in the Indian market.

An arm of the technology giant Satyam, Sify, had acquired Indiaworld.com, with its entire set of properties like Samachar.com, Khel.com and others at a pricey sum. It was for the first time a transaction of this kind had taken place in India, and was supposed to be the largest in the Indian dotcom space. The other big news was that Rediff.com had managed to get listed on NASDAQ.

Besides these, other conversations around valuations were also floating around. We too were in talks with some VCs and were exploring few acquisition opportunities. The promoters and investors felt that the best was yet to come. We felt the same too, hence were not in a hurry to finalise any deal, as we were expecting better ones to come by.

Dotcom Bubble Bursts

While positivity spread like a warm, cosy blanket over the dotcom world, somewhere a small stream of doubt had begun to trickle, which in the long run, would threaten to dampen and soak the interest in the dotcom space. Doubts were being cast over the huge valuations that the dotcom companies had attracted. Netscape was one of the first few companies to get listed on NASDAQ, with fancy valuations. Now, many were questioning that listing and that valuation. Several other dotcom business models had also received huge valuations. But they were unable to get their act together and their business models were failing miserably.

Doubts increased, causing tremors in the West – small ones in the beginning, which gradually led to bigger ones. When one invests heavily, flowing with the hype, and without a thorough understanding of the business, even the slightest instance of trouble can cause panic. This was what was happening. All those who had invested in the dotcom business by simply believing it to be the next big thing, started panicking when business models began to fail. They feared that they would lose all the money they had invested.

As panic increased, wariness crept in. There was a time when everyone wanted to ride the dotcom wave, but with the recent developments, investors were choosing to stay away from it.

Going Gets Tough

Things were not going smooth for us either. We had already spent a fair amount of money that we had raised. Now that everything did

 If I Had To Do It Again...
End of a Fantasy, Back to Reality

not seem rosy in the dotcom paradise, the investors were beginning to get nervous. The international business dailies reported the likely collapse of the dotcoms, and the Indian market anxiously gulped these reports.

It was not just the investors who were wary, but the people who were earlier enthusiastic about associating with us - our advertisers, our vendors - everyone started eyeing the dotcom business with suspicion.

And they had reasons to do so too. For instance, a lot of dotcom companies had invested in building software for their businesses. But now, owing to the mood in the market, they had either abandoned the projects or were unable to pay the software companies to whom they had given expensive contracts. In this manner, many software vendors had burnt their fingers.

This had led to a 'do not touch dotcoms, or you will lose your money' sentiment. And we were a dotcom company. Suddenly, we found people looking at us also with suspicion. Our investors were with us but there was an overall sense of skepticism in the market place.

We were at a juncture, where there was very little money left in the bank, and the prospect of new investors walking in was very bleak. Advertisers, whom we were very dependent on, for generating revenue from the Online Post service, were not very keen to associate with us anymore. Vendors were also not forthcoming to work with us.

Which brought us to a very important question - how do we run the business under these circumstances? There was a huge disaster staring at our face. We had to take stock of the situation and figure out our next step.

When we looked around, people associated with dotcom companies were shutting shop - left, right and center. Many were going back to their old jobs, if they were lucky enough to get them back. We realised we had a major challenge ahead of us.

But there were few silver linings as well. Luckily for us, we had not used up all of the money that we had raised... we still had some left. Sanjay had not yet shifted to the US with his family. Had the family been uprooted and then this realisation that the industry was faltering would have dawned, that would have been a huge blow. Thankfully, that had not happened.

Nevertheless, the road ahead looked very dark. Things were certainly not looking up for us. Some questions came to the mind - did we take right decisions from time to time, or had we faltered on some of the crucial decisions? But the most pressing question was - what were we going to do now? Like other companies, should we also shut shop? Overall, there was a feeling of remorse and we had a tough fight on our hands.

The Wisdom Nugget

> ➤ Markets are either hyper or anti-hyper. Don't get carried away by the market. Reality operates between hype and anti-hype. When there is a lot of hype, the reality is that things actually aren't that brilliant.

 If I Had To Do It Again…
End of a Fantasy, Back to Reality

➤ And when there is anti-hype, the reality is that things actually aren't all that bad. As an entrepreneur keep you feet fairly on the ground and operate your business, based on reality, not on hype.

PART II

2001-2004 :
"Karmanye Vadhika Raste Maa Faleshu Kadachan"

The end of a rollercoaster ride. Coming to the ground with a thud. Back to reality. Back to the basics of business, far away from the emotional highs that we had undergone during the days of the dotcom boom!

That was what we felt in 2001, a little after the realisation that the bubble of the boom had gone bust, and the fanciful dreams remained just that - dreams.

But there was a recognition that what we were doing was fundamentally viable, interesting and a revenue generating opportunity. Not just a play for eye-balls! With that recognition, came a resolve to fight this phase, hard as it appeared to be.

We had no idea how long this phase would last, but we were reasonably convinced that the unique business opportunity we had created for ourselves would grow into a robust and profitable business, sooner or later!

That is what led us to slug it out, knowing clearly well that with the limited funds that we had, and the uncertain future, we could only "do" our deeds, but not really have decent clarity about the actual "results" or "impact." Hence the period is epitomized by the Shloka from Geeta that says, "Karmanye Vadhika Raste Maa Faleshu Kadachan," which means that our focus should be to do our efforts, and not to be obsessed about the results! That is exactly what we ended up doing

 | If I Had To Do It Again…
2001-2004 : "Karmanye Vadhika Raste Maa Faleshu Kadachan"

Chapter 7

To Be or Not to Be

If to Be, Then How to Be: Taking the Call

Negativity had cast a spell around us. The most pertinent thought was – how do we survive? Will we be able to continue the business or not? Should we simply give up and try something else? What is it that we should be doing?

As mentioned before, most of the people around us were winding up their dotcom ventures. A closer look revealed that their businesses revolved solely around the user base and had very little focus on revenue. These websites attracted people through free services like email, gaming, and the like. Once the sites had decent traffic, they created what was referred to as "valuation." The criterion for valuation in those heady days was the number of visitors, rather than the revenue generated. And the best part was that these websites, most of the time, did not have a clue how to generate money. In such a scenario, it was indeed difficult to sustain for a long period – meeting the marketing costs, the overheads, the server costs, the salaries and all that were required to keep their free services going.

Standing Apart

Like them, the Online Post service that we offered was also free, and hence it generated traffic. However, unlike them, we did make good use of the whooping traffic by offering them the Online Gift Store, through which they could send gifts to their near and dear ones in India. Each item that was being sold on the store was priced higher than the amount that we had procured it for. Thus, the Online Gift Store generated revenue for us with a decent gross profit margin. We certainly stood apart from the several other websites that had not given much of a thought to revenue generation.

In order to further strengthen our stand, we pondered on whether our business could have sustained without the Internet. We wanted to understand, if our Online Post service and Online Gift Store had become 'online' just by chance, and if these services could work well without the Internet, in an offline mode.

We came to the conclusion that it was simply impossible for the services to be carried out without the Internet. If it was not for the Internet and the services that we had put together, the NRIs across the world would not have been able to send letters or gifts to their folks in India as and when they needed, and that too at a cheaper rate and in a lesser number of days. This was especially true for smaller cities abroad, where there were fewer NRIs and Indian stores were pretty scarce. In such cases, our Online Gift Store came as a boon. Yes, our business was indeed a pure online venture and there was no way it could survive on an offline mode.

 If I Had To Do It Again…
If to Be, Then How to Be: Taking the Call

We also concluded that we were different from the rest. We had a very interesting and viable online business that was generating decent revenue. No doubt, we were currently undergoing some challenging times, but we were certain that we could survive.

But little did we know that the entire dotcom industry was under scanner, no matter even if one had a viable revenue generating online business. This challenging time was here to stay for a good number of years.

Taking Stock

Now that we were certain we would survive, the next question was how do we move ahead, especially when investors were unlikely to put much money into such businesses now? It was true that we made profits, but we certainly required more money to promote and build our business. We decided to go back to our investors and talk it out.

We must acknowledge here that our investors were extremely supportive and pragmatic, unlike typical VCs, who in similar situations, would have just liked to cut their losses and move on. In fact, there were many such VCs, who upon realising that they had made an incorrect assumption about this industry, were now forcing their investees to wind up the businesses.

In our case, we had got the money from angel investors and not VCs. They supported our point of view and were confident that the business model was viable. While they did not want to put more money into the business at that point of time, they did not force us to close down the business, either.

The reality was also this – even if we had sold off our assets, the investors would have barely got back a tiny fraction of their original investment. Instead if we continued and resurrected our business, without any further dependence on them for money, there was a small chance of possible success. However, they left the decision to us. At that point, if we had thrown up our hands and said we would like to wind up, they would have been okay with that too. But our personal conviction that our business model was viable, dissuaded us from saying so. With complete conviction at our end and a green signal from our investors, we decided to stay put, recognising that it may be a steep and long upward climb from where we were.

Taking Tough Calls

Having taken the decision, we prepared ourselves to face the reality— how much money was left with us and how much more would we need on a month-on-month basis to sustain? How do we balance out the expenses? We had to find ways of making more money at lesser costs - increase the sales, while cutting down the costs. It looked like we had to take some tough decisions.

We had a plush office, which we felt was on the expensive side. As a cost-cutting strategy, we considered moving into a smaller office. The new office was not exactly small, but was at an unenviable location and lacked some basic amenities. We suddenly were working under the hum of the fans – a far cry from the soothing, cool, breeze of the ACs in the previous office.

 If I Had To Do It Again…
If to Be, Then How to Be: Taking the Call

After other such similar administrative cost-cutting, we now turned our focus to the people. There were few people on board whose salaries, at that point, were too much for us to bear. While they had contributed greatly and had played a pivotal role in scaling up the business, we were not in a position to afford them, considering the limited funds that we now had. We had a talk with them. While some agreed on a substantial salary cut and stayed with us, few others chose to move on. This was one of the toughest decisions we took. They were all passionate people and if it was not for the monetary pressure, we would have never liked to lose them. The decision gnawed us for quite sometime but we were helpless. We kept our personal sentiments aside and put the company first. We allowed them to move on.

As they left, we did not even have the money to compensate them on their premature exit. Instead, we showed our appreciation through some small gifts.

By now, we had cut down our team size by about 25 percent, and in terms of salary, we were saving up to 40 percent. The new office reduced our rent by a good margin. At a personal level, as founders, we decided to take a cut in our salaries as well. We were, all the while, taking home nominal salaries, and this cut did not help the situation at all, especially when we had families to support and had to ensure a certain standard of living. But we had no choice and decided to make such entrepreneurial sacrifices - take the cut and manage the show.

Business Resurrection

If cutting down cost by asking people to leave had taken an emotional toll on us, we were in for some more turmoil. Next in line was Online Post service, the service that had actually shaped the business for us, the service that had made us a famous Internet player and enabled us to bag attractive valuations. We had to take a decision – whether to continue or to shut the service completely. Here is why – Online Post was a free service, where NRIs could write letters to folks in India and vice versa. The huge costs incurred in printing letters and sending them locally was covered by advertisements. But with the dotcom bust, advertisers were shy of putting up their advertisements on our website. Now, the entire cost of sending letters fell on our shoulders and was turning out to be a

major cost center. We thought of making it chargeable but realised that it would not work. The only other option would be to shut shop. But we were worried that once this service was stopped, then people may simply stop coming to the Online Gift Store as well. We were not very clear if people visited our site for the free service or whether it was because they were genuinely interested in e-commerce–online gifting. A lot of uncertainty shrouded this decision.

Again, given a choice, we would have loved to continue the Online Post service. But we just did not have the money to support it. In the meantime, what we were anticipating was slowly happening - cybercafés were mushrooming across the country. People with no Internet connection now had an access to it. This, in turn, was slowly stealing the sheen from Online Post service. People were now communicating much faster from cybercafés instead of using Online

 If I Had To Do It Again…
If to Be, Then How to Be: Taking the Call

Post service as the intermediary. In fact, the growth of our user base was slowing down, as cybercafés started growing in number.

Thus, taking everything into consideration, one fine day we decided to put a stop to the Online Post service – the service that had got us everything.

We were very worried that it would have a serious impact on our Online Gift Store, which was now our main cash earner. If people stopped visiting HomeIndia.com as a result of the closure of Online Post service, that would be the end of it all.

To our extreme surprise, there was no drop in the e-commerce traffic. In fact, if anything, it started growing. We simply could not believe it. We were anticipating some drop in traffic but in reality there was none. This brought us to a big conclusion that our e-commerce venture had created a credibility of its own, and people were not reaching the gifting site just because they were lured to it while surfing the free Online Post service. That was a revelation indeed and gave us a lot of satisfaction that the free Online Post service was not actually required to attract traffic. This also meant that we had delivered well – be it letters or gifts – so much so that people kept coming back to our website. With Online Post out of service, there was nothing now to distract people when they visited the website. It had now become a pure e-commerce website and perhaps, this was what was leading to an increase in the traffic.

A successful e-commerce website. That was what we were by the end of 2000-01. Now, our focus was to grow the business on a larger scale. While the decisions that we took in terms of cutting down costs and scaling up our business gave us a certain direction, we were aware of the bigger struggles and the steeper uphill climb that awaited us. We geared up to take on these challenges.

The Wisdom Nugget

➤ When the going gets tough, the tough gets going. Tough times call for tough decisions. And sometimes, taking these tough decisions can be emotionally challenging. Our own learning has been that any decision, which is in the overall interest of the eco-system, is the only right decision and that may sometimes call for measures that we may not otherwise want to take.

➤ One wrong decision, in hindsight, was that we let go some of our senior talent. We should have actually worked hard to retain them. Allowing them to leave created an intellectual bankruptcy at our end, something that would cost us dear in the future.

If I Had To Do It Again…
If to Be, Then How to Be: Taking the Call

Chapter 8

Figuring a Revenue Growth Strategy

With the cleanup drive, we were a smaller team in a cheaper office. We figured out that we may not grow in size anytime soon and neither will we be able to afford appraisals in a hurry. What we could potentially do was to sustain ourselves, at this size.

That was a fresh beginning.

We had been pondering over our next steps for quite some time now. With a smaller team and no marketing budgets, how were we going to scale our business? And if we chose to remain small and not grow, what kind of a company would we be really building? After all, we did expect things to turn around in time, and we wanted to be poised correctly to take advantage at that time?

Thinking and Re-Thinking

We had to go back to the drawing board and think hard about the possible ways and means to grow. Many options were considered.

We looked around for potential partnerships. We checked out if we could ride on bigger brands and become their fulfillment partner. Or get into a tie-up with greeting card companies or other companies that were selling branded Indian products like snacks and groceries to the NRIs. Or maybe get into an alliance with NRI focused dotcoms based in the US. We approached these companies either directly or through our connections. But nothing seemed to stir. Averseness to dotcoms only seemed to grow. From being the poster boys few months back, Internet startups had now become the untouchables of society, or so it appeared.

Moreover, these alliances that we were pondering on seemed to be excellent opportunities from where we stood, but not necessarily a win-win situation for everyone involved. We were in a hurry to find alliances, partnerships or funding options but did not have a clear notion about the value that it would bring to us and the opposite party. It appeared like we were looking for a straw to hold on to survive, but never did we once stop to understand why we wanted the straw and what we would do after we found it. Would it have taken us to a decent goal or taken us out of the woods we were in? We had not even waited to ask these questions, so the answers were never there. Our thoughts were convoluted and that is where we faltered.

Though the alliances did not materialise, we learnt a thing or two. A big learning was that for partnerships or alliances to succeed, it had to be a win-win situation for everyone. Anything less than that would take up lot of effort and time, amounting to nothing substantial.

 | If I Had To Do It Again...
Figuring a Revenue Growth Strategy

Another learning was that depending on others to bail you out of your situation was not exactly a great idea. First, you had to look within, and once you had exhausted all the options, then only might you consider looking outwards to others. This was specially true during stressful times. While in boom, everyone wants to cut a deal and ride on each other's growth or likely growth, but during a bust period, you are your only saviour!

With alliances not materialising, we were back to square one. A sense of frustration was setting in. There was not much to do everyday, besides minding the routine business. And that was not challenging enough. The question, "what next" kept haunting us. We went back to the drawing board yet again, rubbed off everything and decide to start afresh.

The first question that we asked was, "What exactly was our challenge?" Most of the time, there are multiple thoughts, ideas and challenges doing bouts in our head. In a bid to address them all, we often would fail to focus on the real urgency or the prime issue, and may end up with a not-so-apt solution. Right now, we wanted to nail down all our issues. We wanted crystal clear clarity.

We calmly assessed our current position, our key challenges and our immediate constraints.

Our current position:

- We were in a B2C business (Online Gifting Store)

- We were catering to NRI customers

- Our average transaction size was around USD 10

- o Our business was festival oriented

- o Apparel and costume jewelry were our key categories

- o We had the capacity to do a large number of orders

Our key challenges and constraints:

- o We did not have resources for customer acquisition

- o To change the business model from B2C to B2B (Business to Business) would be a huge experiment and would require lot of funds, which was not available with us

- o We quickly needed to grow our revenues to maintain the momentum

This assessment led us to these conclusions:

- o Our revenue was: (Customers) x (number of transactions) x (average transaction size)

- o Out of these three parameters, we could not grow the number of customers to a great extent, due to lack of customer acquisition budgets

- o However, if efforts were put in, we had an opportunity to increase the other two parameters, viz. the number of times the customers transacted with us, and their average transaction size. That would increase our revenues, which was what we were looking for at that time.

This clarity was nearly a Eureka moment for us. Alongside, we also realised that we need not necessarily get into an alliance or

 If I Had To Do It Again…
Figuring a Revenue Growth Strategy

partnership immediately, but could concentrate on increasing the revenue with the resources available with us.

We quickly regrouped our resources. Getting customers to transact more often and increasing the average transaction size became our mantra. It was easier said than done. But at least we had the clarity about the path ahead.

If for a moment, one wonders how this very simple insight around (customers x transactions x average ticket size), came to us so late, it may be appreciated that we came from a very heady period. A period that was characterized with high paced growth, valuations, investments, acquisitions and what not. In that melee, one had somehow lost touch with the basic fundamentals of business. We were just glad to have rediscovered those, and better late than never!

Startling Revelations

The Online Gift Store attracted NRIs who would send gifts to their folks in India, especially during festivals like Diwali and Raksha Bandhan. An analysis of the customer data revealed that the average number of transactions per customer per year was only 1.13. This meant that one person barely did more than one transaction on our site every year. It also meant that we had to keep getting new customers constantly, if we had to sustain the growth. This was an eye-opener for us.

During the dotcom boom, we had never focused on critical details like this. We were busy burning money on advertising, checking out alliances and M&A opportunities. As a result, we had missed out on the basics of a retail B2C business.

Later, there emerged another startling fact. Most of the customers came to shop with us, either during Raksha Bandhan or Diwali. That was the time when we worked with low- priced products and low margins. The whole idea was to acquire customers at low entry points during these festivals, anticipating that we could make our profits when they would come back to shop with us again. But the shocking fact was that they did not come back much! This was indeed a rude wake-up call for us.

We also figured that for a maximum number of our customers, only one of the festivals mattered – either Raksha Bandhan or Diwali. For few others, occasions like weddings, birthdays, and anniversaries were of importance. In all, the concluding fact was that only few of our customers found it important enough to come back and shop with us more than once a year.

This also led to another great revelation - that we were not creating adequate brand loyalty among our customers. It is only when you shop for something every now and then that you remember the brand and the shopping experience. In our case, the customers came to us only on special occasions, which were not close enough to become memorable or to form a genuine brand loyalty. We realised that a person who shopped with us may not necessarily remember us, as his visits were infrequent and he may be getting lured easily by other brands, products, shopping centers or fancy advertisements. We certainly lacked brand loyalty.

 If I Had To Do It Again…
Figuring a Revenue Growth Strategy

The writing on the wall was to go back to the basics, if ever there was one.

Plan of Action

We charted out few points that required our immediate attention:

- We had to understand our customers better

- We had to address their needs better

- We had to improve our brand recall

- We had to ensure that we created transaction opportunities with our customers, more than once a year. We had to ensure that the multiple transaction opportunities actually materialised. For that, we had to have in place a perfect customer communication mechanism.

Armed with these realisations, we began our journey ahead.

Customer Survey

To begin with, we conducted a customer survey – a basic survey. Later on, to keep up the continuity and to understand the trend better, we created an application that would send out a brief survey to the customers within 15 days after their orders had been shipped. The survey had generic questions as well as those related to their specific transactions.

The responses from the survey were constantly viewed and analysed by our top management, the head of CRM and Operations. The feedback was indeed very useful and enabled us to understand our business better, recognise the areas of improvement and plan our future strategies.

We realised that there were two types of customers who gave feedback – first, those who were very happy with our services and second, those who were very unhappy with our services.

It was flattering to read the testimonials, where they praised and appreciated our services. We were proud that we were able to actually deliver emotions through our services and spread happiness. We vowed to do better everyday so as to ensure that the emotions kept flowing seamlessly between people abroad and their near and dear ones in India.

While compliments motivated us to perform better, the complaints showed us our flaws, which were disturbing. There were clear challenges that we faced on a day-to-day basis. When it came to deliveries - vendors, logistics, state rules, road permits, entry taxes, octroi – everything played a crucial role in ensuring successful deliveries. A shortcoming in any one of these factors would lead to a delay in the deliveries. While it was our constant endeavor to overcome these challenges and become a reliable service, these complaints showed that we had to work harder at improving our service quality. Committed as we were to "deliver emotions" and earn customer delight, we tightened our processes to move towards flawless deliveries.

A New Business Opportunity

Through the survey, emerged another business opportunity – something that had never crossed our mind before. We realised that our customers found our products attractive and interesting, and besides sending them to loved ones in India, they showed an impulsive urge to own them themselves. They wanted us to deliver our merchandise to them, wherever they were located.

This feedback was extremely relevant and important, especially when we were pondering on ways to further grow our business. We did an analysis and came up with the following points:

o Gifting happens only during few occasions in a year and is usually budget-driven. While self-purchase can be impulsive, can go beyond budget, and can happen multiple times in a year.

o We had satisfied customers who had been placing gift orders with us. If they migrated to self-purchase, in all likelihood, we would manage to get more transactions from the same customers, instead of acquiring new ones.

o Having already established our credibility through our gifting service, it would be easier to get higher value transactions from our customers through self-purchase, thereby raising the average transaction value per order.

This addressed our two key issues – getting repeat transactions and getting higher value transactions. We were excited about the opportunity that suddenly opened up in front of us.

But then, there were of course, the logistic challenges. As mentioned before, while delivering orders to smaller cities and towns in India, we had faced several challenges in terms of road permit, entry taxes, etc. Now, we were thinking about delivering across the globe. Wouldn't the challenges then simply multiply? Another concern was that we would be receiving orders in small quantities, meaning it would be individual orders and not bulk. In such a case, how feasible would it be to ship one item from India to some far flung city in some corner of the world? The shipping costs would be exorbitant and our landed prices would shoot off the roof. Is such a case, would our products be affordable? Searching answers to all these questions made us realise that a transaction was feasible only if it was happening as smoothly as our domestic transactions.

We started our research to understand how we could smoothly ship our products overseas. We began with studying the courier details and customs laws of different countries, especially that of the US. The US was our biggest market, rest of them would not make much of an impact.

We also started getting shipping rates from various courier companies. At that point, neither did we nor the companies know of the possible volumes of business that we would be able to generate. Hence, the rates that we got were high, but ones which could be reduced later, as soon as we began demonstrating business growth.

We also discovered that there were no serious import restrictions into the US for most of our products. Unless the volumes were large, the shipments could go via a simple retail import route, without a problem. We did need invoices and other such documents,

 | If I Had To Do It Again...
Figuring a Revenue Growth Strategy

but other than those formalities, there were no major issues, we concluded.

The biggest challenge at the moment, we realised, was the high shipping cost, which was likely to increase the landed cost for the buyer. Nevertheless, we decided to go ahead with the service of providing products to NRIs for self-consumption.

Launching International Deliveries

With a view to overcome the challenges, we took some decisions.

Optimising the Costs

We decided to optimise the margins and offer an international delivery price, inclusive of the shipping cost, such that the impact caused by the additional cost was kept to a minimum. In other words, for delivery to international destinations, we did not show the shipping cost separately but added it to the total cost and priced our products at that amount.

However, we realised that it was only products that were priced on the higher side that were able to absorb the shipping costs. In the sense, even after adding the shipping costs, the high-priced products did not appear unusually expensive. But this was not true for products priced at lower rates. These products turned out to be very expensive when the shipping costs were added and we were certain people would not opt for them. Hence, for the lower-priced products, we adopted a different strategy – we bundled them up. We paired them either in twos or fours or numbers like that, such that the products could include the shipping costs and yet not appear too expensive.

US shipping cost treated as the base

Our costing was largely based on the US shipment cost, which in many cases was lower than the shipping cost, to say Australia, or most of the European destinations. The safer option would have been to either offer separate prices based on the country of shipping, or to have taken the highest shipping cost, and worked out our prices with that as a base. This would have ensured that we made more money when some products had to be shipped to destinations with lower shipping costs. However, we were not in favor of either of these options.

Quoting a price for each shipping destination would have complicated the interface for the customer and we did not want that to happen. We could have taken the shipping cost that was the highest amongst the various countries. But why would we do that? If 90 percent of our traffic and orders were from the US (at that time), we had to ensure that we had the costing right for the US deliveries. For other countries, the shipping costs would be a little less or more and accordingly, we would have ended either making or losing some money. In either case, it did not matter. We optimised the prices of our products based on the US shipping cost.

Most Products Up for Delivery

To maintain uniformity across the site, we launched international delivery for almost all our products. The ones that were left behind

 | If I Had To Do It Again…
Figuring a Revenue Growth Strategy

were those that had restrictions on shipment, such as food products and the like.

Terms and Conditions

We also decided to put in fine print the terms and conditions - that customs duty or taxes, if chargeable at the destination, would have to be borne by the customer, as extra. While we did not expect the charges to be applicable in all likelihood, yet we decided to put that line there so that the customers do not start questioning, in some rare cases that they are charged with. We also knew that the custom duty for these small packages may not be a big issue. Even in odd occasions, if the duty was asked for and the customer protested or refused to pay, we would try and pay that from our end itself. We did not want to scare the customers away. We wanted to sell first. We wanted our customers to see a clear landed price at their doorsteps, with no sudden surprises. After taking these decisions, we went ahead to launch our international shipping service.

Before we move ahead, let us go back to the pricing bit once again.

The Pricing Tactic and All that Went into It

When we included shipping charges on the products meant for international delivery, the rates actually looked quite high. For example, an art silk sari costing

USD 25 for delivery within India, was working out to be USD 45 on international delivery. Or a Ganesh idol for USD 15 within India was working out to USD 25 when shipped outside India.

The thought of keeping the shipping cost as extra, based on the destination, actual weight and cost, had crossed our mind. In which case, the bundling that we did for low-priced products would not have been required. The customers would have themselves discovered that adding more items to their shopping cart made for better efficiency on the shipping costs.

However, at that time, the conviction that we carried and which we boldly proclaimed on our site was that the price that the customers saw on the site was the price that they paid - nothing more, nothing less. In short, we wanted to tell them that we were different! Unlike some of the other sites that offered e-commerce during that period, where the final amount worked out to be a lot more than the basic amount visible on the site, thanks to the shipping, handling, taxes, etc.. In our case, the customers saw the actual final amount that they had to pay, for door delivery of their order! That being the logic, we decided to stick to our all-inclusive prices, and hence we added the shipping cost to the cost of product.

Many years later, we would change our minds and shift to a policy where shipping charges were added later, based on the weight and volume of the products purchased. This is only to validate the point that in a startup business, or in an entrepreneurship journey, or perhaps in life itself, nothing is permanent, and you never say "never!!!"

That had to come later, but now, as we launched our international delivery segment, we still winced at the cost of the products. Knowing the original costs did not help us in any way. We had some serious questions regarding our pricing - would the customers find

 | If I Had To Do It Again…
Figuring a Revenue Growth Strategy

our prices palatable or would they be put off and withdraw from our site? In such a case, would it damage our brand? Would a stray customer in Singapore wonder why she was getting products at the same price as those being delivered to her cousin in Chicago?

The urge to address all the questions was irresistible, even if the questions were still only on our minds, and the customers had not even got close to raising them. We wanted to explain why we were priced high, why there was a difference in the India and the international delivery rates, the reason behind the single pricing for international deliveries.

In such over-defensive situations, people tend to react even before the need arises. Thankfully, we did not give into the temptation. If we had, we would have cluttered the site and made it very confusing for the customer. Good sense prevailed and we waited for the customers' reactions, before we put up our over-defensive sounding explanations.

We need not have feared. The customers took the rates in their stride. We realised that the customers did not worry much. They liked our simplicity and our 'KISS' philosophy – Keep It Simple and Straightforward!

Having said that, things may be slightly different for a B2B business, where you may be sitting across the table and addressing the concerns on a one-on-one basis. However, for a B2C, you simply have to figure out the common denominator customer, the average buyer who visits your site and try to address your communication keeping that customer in mind. In case of any doubt, you may choose to lean towards the simpler rather than the complex. If need be, you can add the complexities later.

Response to International Deliveries Makes Us Happy

Before we talk about the reaction to the products meant for international deliveries, let us quickly dwell into a range of products that we had once added to our gifting segment and the skepticism that had surrounded them.

We had introduced ethnic apparel like saris, churidar, kurtas, salwar kameez, etc as gift items on HomeIndia.com. These did not come in any standard size and we were very skeptical as to whether these products would move. We were not sure if Indian ladies would purchase apparel online because they are so used to trying on the clothes several times before deciding on what to purchase, and sometimes even after several trials, they would end up picking none. In such a scenario, would people buy apparel based simply on web images and descriptions?

We were in for a pleasant surprise as this section started picking up very well and quickly emerged as our single largest gifting category, other than festival shopping.

Similarly, when we introduced the self-purchase section meant for the NRIs with our own doubts about the pricing and other factors, we were again in for a pleasant surprise. People started picking up products almost right from the day that we launched this offering. They did not have any issues and were ready to buy the products at the prices that were offered to them.

 If I Had To Do It Again…
Figuring a Revenue Growth Strategy

We need not have worried about the pricing anyway, because, later, after many discussions with the customers, we realised a couple of things.

- o The price that a customer pays has nothing to do with its manufacturing cost or the purchase price. It is the value that he sees in the product that matters. In our case, the customers saw so much value that the rates did not matter to them much. Moreover, the products were attractive and there were no other easy options available to them to procure the same, as NRIs may not necessarily have Indian stores close to where they lived. Here, we were giving them the option to choose from a large range of attractive offerings, and shop comfortably from the comfort of their homes, without worrying about packaging or shipping or any other such logistics.

- o If we compare the effort put and the time spent in shopping online, it definitely would be lesser than taking time out during weekends and visiting stores located at far flung areas.

- o In case we compare the prices, the products at the stores too were priced quite high. In fact, they had a simple pricing strategy - after importing their products to the US, the vendors would calculate the landed cost and multiply it over three to five times. In fact, our pricing turned out to be cheaper than what they would get at these local stores.

Taking all these factors into consideration, HomeIndia.com came across as a boon to the NRIs. No wonder that the store picked up business right from day one. It also helped that we had dwelled deep into the issues that might have cropped up during the international deliveries, and had already set up the terms and conditions to address them. Our international delivery segment was certainly on the roll.

Opening of Additional Business Channels

With the launch of products for international deliveries, we noticed a certain trend picking up. In the earlier days, as a gifting site, our focus had been mainly on festivals. While Raksha Bandhan and Diwali drove in huge volumes of business, the rest of the year remained quite flat. We were heavily skewed towards seasonal business.

As India is a land of festivals, we had tried to cater to more festivals like Gudi Padva, Sankrant, Lohri, etc and had tried to inculcate a habit of gifting among the people during these festivals. However, our efforts bore little fruit because the gifting orders that we received during some of these other festivals were not even worth mentioning. We realised that it was not possible to change the fundamental habit of the customers, where they believed in gifting only during major festivals. For instance, Valentine's Day had become a significant shopping and gifting occasion, thanks to the coordinated efforts of many brands and media houses, who endorsed and promoted the 'Day.' But in case of the other numerous festivals in India, it was a tedious task to get people to gift. At least, it was not possible for a lone brand like ours to achieve it.

But with the launch of the international deliveries, we noticed an interesting trend beginning to take place. A Maharashtrian gentleman in Seattle may not think of sending gifts to his families or relatives during a Gudi Padva, but he may consider it an apt occasion to buy a new sari for his wife. And if he had an option to book it online and receive the sari at his doorstep, what more could he ask for? In this manner, the business began to pick up during various festivals, opening up additional business channels for us. Now, our focus turned to this segment and we started working on a suitable communication strategy for our customers.

Communicating with Customers

We were already sending mails to our customers, reminding them of the products available on Homeindia.com. But the communication was quite standard and since we were emailing to about a lakh of people, we did it with lot of caution so as not to abuse the list. Hence, the mails that we sent out were not very frequent. However, the opening up of this new opportunity to sell products all the year round gave us more reasons to frequently send the emails now. We developed a multi-pronged email strategy.

We sliced our email database into some simple forms, so that we could send targeted emails to the sliced groups. Like for instance, sari buyers could get emails whenever we introduced a new range of saris or a particular community could receive details about different products as their festivals approached.

It was not an easy task because we did not have many details about our customers. Registration was not mandatory for shopping on HomeIndia.com. If at all a person registered with us, we took very minimal data from him.

The logic being - when a person walked into our store with an interest to shop, why hinder him with an elaborate registration process? Moreover, did we actually need registration? Our conviction told us that registration was not very important. What was important was to make the store easily accessible for the customers and to give them a hassle-free shopping experience. Using that logic, even if a person registered with us, not much emphasis was laid on getting a detailed registration.

Hence, we had very limited details about our customers. Our database slicing was mainly based on their shopping history – the categories they had shopped for, the number of times they had shopped, the price points and the like. Based on these data, we planned our email campaigns, which included designing attractive communication, deciding on the number of products to be included, and zeroing down on the target audience. We also managed to standardise our emails so that people could instantly recognise our mails.

Over the years, as we ran the email campaigns frequently, we achieved a better understanding of the customers' behavior and were easily able to interpret the outcome of email marketing. The campaigns enabled us to analyse what was working and what was not. After a mail was sent to a specific target group, we would track the customer behavior for about a week, the links that got clicked, and the number of times that the links got clicked. In this manner, we were able to analyse the format that worked, and the products that generated the most interest.

Another important aspect we learnt was to leave the site uncluttered. Website owners always have this undying urge to communicate

 | If I Had To Do It Again…
Figuring a Revenue Growth Strategy

constantly with their customers and empty spaces usually tempt them to put up some sort of communication or promotional offers. But the reality is that it does not work. Users usually fleet through the web pages. They land on a page and quickly notice few things that may or may not work for them. In case, it works, the user would stay and perhaps navigate to the inner pages. In case it does not work, the user clicks the back button and is out of the site even before you notice. Hence, in terms of communication, you can identify the 'one' best thing that you wish to communicate to the customer and keep that prominently on the site. It would work wonders. In case you have five things to communicate, stick to only five, even if there is ample space for you to say more. Just because you have the space and you try to pack a 100 things, then there is a good chance that a visitor won't notice the important aspects.

The interesting bit about online business is that everything can be monitored, unlike an offline business. When you advertise in the offline space, you may not be able to match a response to a specific advertisement. For instance, you might not be able to suggest who responded to a specific spot on television or to a particular hoarding at a certain location or a certain print advertisement. For that matter, even in direct marketing campaigns, it was difficult to understand the rate of response, unless the customer was willing to divulge that he is responding to a letter received from you.

However, in an online business, it was completely the opposite. You could monitor almost everything. Everything was a hyperlink away and there were 'cookies' that revealed customer behavior. Over the years, various improved analytic options have kept throwing fantastic analyses. One such tool was the Google Analytics, a free service offered by Google and perhaps the best tool at that time. An amazing product, it gave us tons of information about the users - right from the time they landed on our site to their exit.

The Wisdom Nugget

➤ Our solution to our challenges did not come from an external source. It came from within. No outsider knows your business better than you do!

➤ In Physics, when we have to solve a complex problem, we would go back to the basics. The term used to describe this process is called "ab-inito," which literally, when translated, means "from the beginning." Likewise, when faced with a serious business crisis, you need to go back to the grass roots, decode each piece of the puzzle and put it back together to create a new formation or a new opportunity.

➤ Also while our business evolved from Online Post to Online Gifting and now to Online Shopping, we kept the basic brand DNA intact...HomeIndia.com's DNA - that of 'bridging an emotional gap.' The core of the business or purpose must remain...even while everything outside and around can change.

If I Had To Do It Again...
Figuring a Revenue Growth Strategy

Chapter 9

Can't Outsource?

Then, Build Your Own: About Supply Chains

We majorly dealt in ethnic Indian products. They were either handmade or procured from cottage industries, while few were manufactured. They were not standardised and neither came in packed boxes nor with any brand name. Whether these were handicraft items, sarees, salwar kameez or jewellery, none of these could be identified as structured SKU (stock keeping units) that one would normally find in an organised retail business.

How We Procured the Products

When we launched our Online Gifting Store, we would go to local retailers for these products. We would take pictures of the products available with them, add brief descriptions and upload them on HomeIndia.com. As far as the rates were concerned, we added our margin to the amount that the retailers offered them to us. It worked well, because when the rates got converted into dollars, it did not amount to much. Moreover, we did not expect our NRI customers to make a comparison between the rates listed on the site and their original cost in the Indian market.

When we received orders for these items, we would go to the retailers to procure the same. The retailers would keep aside a certain amount of stock, exclusively for us. As the orders were not very large in numbers, the retailers were able to hold stock and supply the products easily. This was how we operated the gift store, comfortably.

But now, the situation was different. With the launch of international deliveries, we were not very clear about the order quantity. Even if we asked the retailers to keep aside a certain quantity of stock, what if the orders were more than that? We would be running helter-skelter for procurement, and in case we did not find the products, our reputation would be at stake. Certainly, not a nice situation to be in. Moreover, as the store grew in size, we would have to offer larger variety of items. And not all of them would move at the same rate. In such a case, if we ask the retailers to keep aside some stock of all the items that they offered us, and if several items did not get sold, they would not be happy either. Their inventory would remain blocked, and later on when they tried to sell the excess inventory, the items may not be in demand. Due to all these reasons, there was a challenge to get the retailer suppliers to keep aside a decent stock of items for us.

At our end, we did not want to take a chance, especially when we were planning to introduce other interesting products, apart from those existing on the site. We realised that it was critical for us to find a mechanism, where we would have a regular supply of the

 If I Had To Do It Again…
Then, Build Your Own: About Supply Chains

products. It was also important for us to reduce our costs and increase the profit margin. One way of doing this was by procuring the products at a cheaper rate – perhaps by directly approaching the distributors or manufacturers, instead of the retailers. We decided to go deeper into the supply chain and explore its feasibility.

Soon, we realised that approaching the manufacturers and retailers was a good idea, but it had its own share of issues. For instance, if we wanted to procure ready products, for example sarees, there were two issues involved:

- First, unlike a retailer, the manufacturer would expect us to place large orders. Now, when we were not very sure of the size of the orders, how do we decide on the quantity to be procured?

- Second, he would not keep aside the sarees or other such products. Instead, he would want us to take them away with us. This meant that we create some storage space and get onto inventory management.

The silver lining in all this was that we were getting the products at half the rate that we used to pay to the retailer suppliers.

We had to take a decision – buy products at half the cost from manufacturers and distributors and stock them as our inventory, or continue to buy products from the retailers at 50 percent more and not be worried about the storage issues. We decided to go with the former. After all, we were getting the products cheaper and it also ensured that we had a decent quantity at our disposal.

The only catch, rather the risk, in this case was that we might get stuck with the products if they don't sell. We decided to play it safe. To test the waters, we began by procuring products in small quantities. The moment we received the

orders and the stock was over, we removed the products from our site. While it reduced our risks, it also allowed us to understand our customers' behavior.

We began to understand their buying pattern during festivals and otherwise - the kind of products they liked to purchase, their response to certain products, their preferred colours and types. This helped us predict our required volumes better. For example, if we understood that a red saree with a certain kind of style and border was what people preferred, we knew that if we would get more variety of the same kind, most of these would sell well. In this manner, we kept learning and, in turn, sharpening our accuracy at predicting the volumes that we would genuinely need.

Of course, it could never be precise and it could never be that our stocks moved hundred percent every time. Whenever, we had extra stock in hand, we would announce a end-of-season sale or some promotional offer, similar to what retailers would have done in their shops. We knew that whenever we put up discounts, the stocks were quite likely to get picked up. In case the products still failed to move, then we would give them away as incentives. For instance, we would give away an item priced at USD 25 as an incentive with an item worth USD 200. We basically used the USD 25 priced product to make the USD 200 priced item appear more attractive. These were traits of the retailing world that we were picking up.

 If I Had To Do It Again…
Then, Build Your Own: About Supply Chains

In fact, we were forced to learn these traits quickly because we had inventory in hand that had to move. In case, we had chosen not to maintain the inventory, then we might have announced these promotional offers only as a marketing ploy. Now, it was marketing to clear the inventory, which worked very well, and we rarely ended up with dead stock.

Creating Niche Products

While people were buying our products for self-consumption and the segment was performing decently, it was still the festivals that generated maximum business for us. Considering this fact, we had to nurture the festival / gifting / segment better. Initially, we had only put items that were clearly festival - oriented, such as typical Indian sweets during Diwali or a Rakhi thali during Rakshabandhan. But soon, competitors began to catch up with us. If a competitor sold a box of Kaju Katli for USD 9.95, there was little chance that we could sell it for USD 15. At the most, we could sell it for about USD 10.95. This was then putting a cap on our sales. The only way out was to come up with innovative products. And we did just that. Here is how.

When you go out into the streets during Diwali, you are likely to notice lanterns and torans, and such other fancy decorations. If you estimate the actual cost of these products, they probably will not be more than five to ten rupees. After all, it consists of some paper and thermocol but they are sold probably ten times more the price, at Rs 100. We were inspired by these products and soon learnt that it was necessary to have products that cost low but were valued high in perception. From a simple trade point of view, if we had thought of procuring the decorative items, the seller might have sold us a product at Rs 50, and we might have sold it further at Rs 150. But in case, we created the product at Rs 10 and sold it at Rs 150, the gross margin suddenly became very exciting. But for that, we had to dirty our hands in making the products ourselves and maybe involve some middle men who would take a cut from our profits.

We decided to take on the responsibility of creating the products but without the middle men. We began by developing products for every season and, surprisingly, we came up with some fantastic items. We suddenly came to be known for our creativity, as we were providing products that were not available anywhere, not even on the Indian streets.

One such product was the Rakhi Patrika. Made of handmade paper, which was colourful and rich in texture, the product looked like a box and had five sheets within, each of which had lovely messages from a sister to a brother, or vice versa. We had developed the messages from the heart and they immediately struck a chord with the customers, especially in the cases of long-distance brother-sister relationships, where one of the siblings was an NRI. Along with the messages, we added tilak, rice and many other puja items, and completed it off with Shree and Om embellishments. The end product looked rich, traditional, and seemed to actually carry the pure and beautiful emotions of a brother and a sister.

The creation of this product would have costed us about Rs 35 to Rs 40, and we were able to sell it for Rs 500 to Rs 750. Sometimes, we combined it with a box of sweet and sold it for Rs 1000. That

If I Had To Do It Again…
Then, Build Your Own: About Supply Chains

was a very good margin indeed. Buoyed by the success of exclusive products, we began creating Diwali thalis, Puja thalis, interesting diyas, and other decorative items with a lot of impressive designs. All these were fresh creations and were an instant hit with the customers.

The design was the key. We had highly creative people who could understand the emotional connect behind these festivals and could accordingly come up with concepts and ideas. We sourced the materials directly, and recruited people who could develop the products. This was how we managed to make some really fantastic products.

Handling the Inventory

During festival seasons, we had to produce huge quantities of these products. Again, we were not sure of the number of orders that might pour in. We had to stock the products because it was not feasible to develop them at the last moment. Sometimes, it so happened that we would develop 3000 units and we would receive orders for only 2000. Or, sometimes the entire 3000 would get picked up a week before Diwali and we would be left with no products during the last week, which, in turn, would force us to put up the 'out of stock' sign during peak season.

In case we were stuck with the products, like the 1000 mentioned above, we had no option but to hold them for a complete year – till next Diwali. This situation came with its own set of challenges. We had to ensure that the extra products were packaged and stored extremely well, lest they were exposed to moisture and began to look old by next season or they became easy prey for rodents, etc. We had to keep the products intact so that we could sell them next year. Repeat customers may have remembered them, but there were many new customers who came in each year, for them, these would work well as these products would appear as whole new products altogether. This was how we managed, and only in some odd cases did we suffer the loss of inventory. In such cases, our margins made up for it. That was what the whole inventory rigmarole was all about.

Another Interesting Business Opportunity

While festivals did extremely good business, we were still pondering on how we could get the customers to spend more – increase their transaction size. Clothing or fashion apparel was a key segment, where people spent a lot of money. Could we then introduce custom-made clothes for our customers, as part of the international deliveries section? Custom-made could be a customised design as per a customer's needs, or an existing design fitted to a custom size, instead of the "standard" size only.

Whenever you visit a store, you come across standard sizes only, in which you may or may not fit. In such cases, at least in India, you may find a neighbourhood tailor to fix it and give you the perfectly fitted dress, but the case may not be the same outside India. In the West, anything that needed to be custom-made was either not available at all or was very expensive. And when it came to Indian clothing, did "custom-made" even exist at all in those countries? We thought not. It soon dawned on us that there indeed was a clear business opportunity in offering custom-made Indian clothing to people outside India. This could be an add-on to the products that we were already selling on the site. For example, a saree on the site could be accompanied with a custom-made blouse.

We thought of giving it a shot. There was a huge amount of work involved in getting clothes custom-sized. We approached fashion designers and asked them what all went into getting customised dresses. They gave us details of the specifications they wanted from the customers. Based on that, we developed an online form, which the customers could fill – like the measurements, the design they desired, and such other details. These online forms were then passed on to outsourced designers, who would stitch the clothes and send them back to us. We, in turn would send them to the customers. We thought it would work well. But soon, customers were coming back to us, utterly dissatisfied. They were unhappy with either the fittings or the designs or other such issues. In such cases, we would go back to the designers. But they would simply throw up their hands and say that they had done exactly what was specified. We were caught in between and had to pay a heavy price – a growing base of dissatisfied customers! We had serious customer service issues in hand and wondered how we could overcome them.

We sensed that while the opportunity was there, we were missing something, somewhere. We had to find the gap and fill it.

We realised that there was a clear communication gap between the customers and the designers. We, as intermediaries between both of them, had no clue about designing and the specifications that we were making the customers fill. The only solution was to have a smooth communication flow between both the parties. To enable this, we decided to hire a small team of designers ourselves, whose fundamental role would be to understand the customers' requirements and convey the same to the outsourced designers. Suddenly, from being an online retailer, we were on our way to becoming a fashion boutique. Once an opportunity was identified, we found a way of making things happen!!

This move completely changed the business opportunity. First of all, the designers improved our online specification form. They asked the right questions and took in more details like the height, weight and so on. They even asked about the seams – whether in or out and such other critical details. We realised it was very easy to take measurements of a person walking into a store, but doing it online and trying to get it perfect was indeed a different ball game altogether.

With everything happening online, our designers would sometimes chat with the customers or call them up. Or at times, they would even sketch the design and send it to the customers to ensure that they had got it right. By the end of it, our designers would have understood exactly what the customers wanted. Later, they would give the specifications to the vendors who stitched them for us. When we got the stitched clothes, our designers would again confirm if they had met the exact requirements. In this manner, we were able to give our customers custom-made clothes - exactly the way they wanted them. It was a huge success and we were flooded with appreciation mails.

 | If I Had To Do It Again…
Then, Build Your Own: About Supply Chains

This success made us more ambitious. If we could manage simple blouses and salwar kameez, could we try our hand at more exclusive and expensive dresses like a custom-made bridal wear with heavy hand-made embroidery or a high-end party wear? That would easily sell for anything between the range of USD 1000 to 3000, thus increasing our transaction size. Could we do it?

We thought we could and thanks to our designers, we actually did. From there on, we constantly upped our product offerings and the quality. Most of the services were outsourced, and we were able to scale the business well.

The point we are making is that we had challenges, but the challenges brought along with them opportunities to innovate, which we did. The challenge of not having the desired cash flow forced us to think of out-of-the-box ways and means to grow our volumes. In the process of increasing volumes, we went on to increase the profit margin by going deeper into the supply chain and stocking our own inventory. We soon learnt how to overcome the challenges of supply chain management and also came up with some fantastic, exclusive products to create a brand niche for ourselves. We also successfully managed to get better margins. In a bid to increase the transaction size, we moved on to making high-end custom-made clothes for our customers, which required us to hire specialist fashion designers. When the designers came on board, the whole business took a turn and we were able to increase the set of offerings and create high value products, which then took the business to the next level.

The Wisdom Nugget

- ➤ One has to have an open mind to evolve and respond to the market needs. When we started the business, it was supposed to be a branding game built on technology skill-set. However as the business model evolved and we felt the need to master supply-chains, we went ahead and did exactly that.

- ➤ As mentioned earlier, as long as the core of the business remains the same, everything else around it could continue to change

 If I Had To Do It Again…
Then, Build Your Own: About Supply Chains

Chapter 10

Friends and Advisors

The Value of Feedback

Pausing the story of our entrepreneurial journey for a moment, we would like to briefly turn our focus on the value of having the right friends and advisors when one is launching a venture. Believe us! They play a critical role.

If you remember, we were engineers, hailing from a traditional business background and we had started off our venture in a domain where we did not have much expertise – the Internet. We had our tryst with Internet only during our college days, and our business was launched about a decade after that. Despite Internet not being our core strength, we decided to launch Internet seminars. Somehow, we had the good wisdom to approach friends - like Ketan Sanghvi and Shuvam Mishra - who were experts in the Internet domain. We openly discussed our challenges and they helped us with ideas to overcome them. Internet seminars were quite a hit. Had we not approached them, this success would not have been possible.

The reason why we are making this point is because we keep meeting entrepreneurs on a daily basis and our frequent observation has been that most of them are reluctant to meet people or discuss their business ideas. We personally feel that this is not healthy and that an entrepreneur cannot afford to be an introvert. If anything, an entrepreneur is a missionary and should always behave like he is on a mission. In fact, he should not even have the hesitation to get potentially insulted, at times. His mission, his venture is what should matter at the end of the day, even if that means meeting dozens of people and discussing his business idea.

Most of the time, entrepreneurs are reluctant to talk to people because of the unfounded fear that their 'secret business idea' may get stolen. Or, they may be battling the hesitation of – how do I ask? It often feels like a big burden to ask somebody for any kind of guidance, forget help or asking for money. Even for general guidance, there is a sense of hesitation that is quite prevalent among entrepreneurs.

Let us first tackle the fear of a business idea being stolen. The reality is that if your business is all about an idea, and not about anything else, then it is a non-starter, anyway. Your success is rarely going to be on account of an idea, rather it is far more about the execution – an aspect that you would not be giving away to anybody when you go to discuss an idea. On the flip side, if you don't discuss, you might be missing out on some serious value-addition that somebody could impart on account of their experience. By asking a person candidly for advice, you are taking advantage of that person's experience and saving yourself of going through that much of a learning cycle.

Well, we did go out and ask friends and advisors for guidance, all the time! As we grew in our business, we looked up to friends and advisors at every juncture. Here are few instances:

 | If I Had To Do It Again…
The Value of Feedback

E-Commerce

When we were venturing into e-commerce, we had to buy products. We were no traders or retailers or shop owners and had no clue about what products to procure and how. When we thought of jewellery, we first went to some friends who dealt in jewellery business in India. Through them, we learnt about how this market functioned and the likely challenges that it might pose. Similarly, when we wanted to sell sarees, we went to a family relative who had a saree shop, and who, later, turned out to be the initial supplier for us.

Advertising

When we decided to invest the money that we had raised on brand building, we did not have much idea on how to go about it. We had never indulged in advertising before. But we knew that we were going to spend a huge amount of money and had to urgently figure out the correct positioning of our brand. We also knew that a significant part of our growth depended on the success of our advertising campaigns. We pondered deeply on factors like - what should be our communication? Should it be simple or elaborate? How should our logo look? Should it have a tag line? What colours should we be using? Moreover, we were planning to advertise in the US. For that, we had to zero down on the right TV channels, the apt days and the best slots. As we treaded into these new areas, we turned to our friends who gave us valuable inputs.

Venture Capital

Likewise, when we were raising funds, we were locked in a situation with two investors, whom we were not particularly comfortable with. However, with no other choice, we had to choose one of them. Given the seriousness of the situation, we went to a friend for guidance. And as fate would have it, through that friend, we located a third investor who finally ended up investing in our venture, and we were saved from picking up from the two uncomfortable options. If we had not approached that friend, the opportunity would have never surfaced.

Tapping the Knowledgebase

The point to understand here is that, as you are growing your entrepreneurial venture, you will be faced with different set of challenges everyday - problems

that you had not foreseen yesterday or issues that are not from your area of expertise. At the same time, you would realise that you know people who may have the knowledge to solve them. In such a case, why not go and tap them? Surprisingly, you may find that friends and well-wishers are happy to spend time with you and give you the guidance. It is only when you get too pesky that they start avoiding you. So, take care to be polite and not to overstay your welcome, while seeking guidance. Having said that, at times, people may shrug you off, or worse, insult you. Just develop a thick-skin to take all these in your stride, after all you are on a mission.

 | If I Had To Do It Again...
The Value of Feedback

Building Your Network

While we are talking about seeking advice, it is also important to know enough people who can potentially help. In other words, one has to have a strong personal network. Today, online social platforms are playing an important role in this case. Besides the people one knows personally, these platforms help widen one's circle by enabling them to easily connect with a lot of other people - both at a personal and a professional level. LinkedIn is a classic example, when it comes to enhancing professional network. It is an effective platform to reach out to people, especially when one is looking around for professional advice to solve some business related issues.

For instance, let us say that you are setting up an office outside India and want to understand its related tax implications. Ideally, you may turn to your friends or contacts but in case there are no experts there, would your contacts on LinkedIn be of help? However, you are not sure who exactly in your contact list is related to this field. It is difficult to individually scan through the 300 to 400 contacts to see who fits the bill. In such a case, all you have to do is look for international taxation experts on LinkedIn. In all probability, either the person may be directly your contact, or may be connected to one of your contacts on LinkedIn. You will find your 'degree of connection' to that person. For example, the person may be just two degrees away from you, meaning you have a friend who knows the expert. In such a case, you simply have to ask your friend to introduce the two of you to take the conversation ahead. Isn't that quick and simple?

The idea is to build up your personal network so that when the time comes, you can use it to reach out to the right people.

Rotary Clubs for Networking

In addition to virtual networks, we also found organisations like the Rotary Clubs to be very useful. Rotary Clubs have members from all walks of life - different educational backgrounds, professions and businesses. Being part of it, you enjoy a good comfort zone with all the members, and whenever you need help or advice, you can approach them and they are very open to pitch in. Both of us have been members of the Rotary Club for many years and have found this network to be extremely useful. It is not about exploiting your friendship or connections for business help, but it is just a good place to turn to because you have friends there who will help you easily.

Seek Help, Help Others

Like we mentioned before, networking and connecting with people offers tremendous value to an entrepreneur. Take the benefit of **others'** experience, rather than to depend on your own. Keeping fears and insecurities at bay, one must relentlessly reach out to people for help and guidance, whenever and wherever required. To grow their businesses better and faster, we would strongly recommend fellow entrepreneurs to build a robust network, seek help, and make sure that your journey includes somebody else's experience as well, and not just your own.

 If I Had To Do It Again…
The Value of Feedback

Also, we must emphasize that networking is a two-way street. Be equally willing to help others when they need your expertise. In fact, it is always a good idea to build your credit balance first. What that means is that first do the good karma of helping others, and don't keep the count. Networking is not a give-and-take barter transaction. The balancing happens over time. Take note that the balancing may not happen with the same person. You give to someone, and take from someone else. It is a concept of paying-it-forward. Rather than paying back. That way you keep the overall ecosystem of doing good to others, going. You keep the good karma flowing!

The Wisdom Nugget

➤ As mentioned earlier, all of us are blessed with a network of friends, relatives, acquaintances and business colleagues. As an entrepreneur, we must learn to reach out into this network and seek guidance and support, where necessary.

➤ Don't be shy of knocking the doors. Knock as many doors as you can (when needed.) Some will open. And some won't. But of the ones that do open, some may contribute significant enlightenment in your entrepreneurial journey.

➤ However, do bear in mind that this eco-system of friends and acquaintances needs to be nurtured. And while they will give you guidance and advice and benefit of their experience, don't expect them to carry your burden. You need to carry your own burdens. Also, it is clearly a matter of give-and-take. Just that you may take from someone and give it to someone else. You keep the ball rolling. Help others, when you can. That is the essence of networking, which is also the essence of being a part of the entrepreneurial ecosystem.

Chapter 11

Bollywood and Internet

Potent Combination for Global Reach

In a bid to increase the transaction size and the number of transactions, we ventured into high-end apparel segment, where we began offering exclusive custom-made dresses. The price of these dresses ranged from Rs 12,500 to Rs 75,000 per piece, and people were happy to purchase them.

This price band was indeed much higher, compared to a typical sale of a book or a music CD - the most popular items on other ecommerce portals during those times - where each piece sold at about Rs 200 to 300. On the other hand, with such high end fashion products, we ended up doing Rs 50,000 per piece kind of transactions. What also made this a big win for us was the fact that our customers trusted us and were ready to purchase high-valued products from us, on the basis of what we presented on the website. We, in turn, focused on robust processes and hundred percent reliable deliveries.

With this line of business, also came the realisation that high-end ethnic fashion wear demanded a price that people were willing to pay, and we could own that category in the online world.

Bollywood – a Major Inspiration

High-end fashion wear is about design. Initially, when we created our own designs, we had to figure out what would be popular with our international audience, who were largely based in the US and Europe. What kind of designs would appeal to them? What style would inspire them? Or rather, where did our customers draw their inspiration from when it came to style and design? Very quickly, we came to the conclusion that it was the Indian entertainment sector. Through this sector, our customers formed an impression about what made a good, contemporary fashion statement. Entertainment included both - films (Bollywood) and Television.

How did We Come to this Conclusion?

In the due course of building our business, we had made several trips to the US. On one such visit, we chanced to be at an Indian store during a weekend. What we saw there was quite interesting. Many NRIs were walking in with video cassettes of the then very popular Hindi TV serial - 'Kyunki Saas Bhi Kabhi Bahu Thi.' They would walk in with a particular cassette number of the serial (covering a bunch of episodes) and walk away with the next cassette, covering the subsequent few episodes of the serial. We realised that those Indian stores there were diligently renting out sequential episodes of the serial and making them available to the NRIs. The NRIs,

 If I Had To Do It Again…
Potent Combination for Global Reach

in turn, were ardently watching the serials during the weekends –
300 episodes, and they were still going strong. This was the impact
Indian TV serials had on the NRIs. Over time, many such TV serials
had become popular among the NRIs. Then, of course, there was
Bollywood. We were told by Indian fashion store owners in the US
that whenever a new Hindi film was released, people would surge
into their stores and ask for fashion items similar to what they saw
in the film. They wanted them right there and then!

Our Learning

What we learnt from TV, especially from the long running soap
operas, was that the NRI viewers were able to see the evolution of
a character on the screen and with it, the evolution of what that
character was wearing. When a soap opera ran for two to three
years, the characters on the screen would wear different attire and
jewellery. This, to the NRI, would be an indicator of the changing
fashion in India. It was under the influence of these changes that
they would change their own preferences about what they wanted to
wear - the colour, style, accessory, embroidery, and the like.

Similarly, Bollywood was evergreen and ever popular among the
NRIs, wherever they were around the world. Even in areas where
there were not many Indians to justify an Indian store, Hindi
movies and music reached them – either in the form of mail order,
cassettes, online downloads or whichever way. Bollywood was the
NRIs' biggest draw in terms of entertainment, and the supply chain
– formal or informal - ensured that their appetite for Hindi movies
and songs was regularly satiated, somehow or the other.

From locations where Indians were present in very small numbers, like the Fiji Islands to areas where they had a huge presence like Chicago, New York and Los Angeles, Indians were consuming Indian TV and Bollywood content for sure. That was the conclusion we drew. And besides providing the undoubted entertainment value to NRIs the world over, these entertainment channels were giving them a sense of the popular Indian fashion, of the times.

Custom-Made Bollywood Dresses

When we were creating custom-made designer wear for people, they would often send us images of dresses worn by celebrities or stars in certain films, and ask us if we could make exact replicas for them?

Initially, we approached this opportunity by offering custom-designed clothing. Our slogan was "Give us some design you love, and we will custom-make it for you and deliver it to you."

Over time, as these requests kept coming, we reckoned that there was an opportunity where we could actually offer Bollywood-inspired apparel. What we meant was that, on the website, we would put images of a star wearing a certain kind of a dress, especially ethnic Indian wear – it could be male or female attire - and we would offer to custom-fit that dress for the customer.

This was an entirely different concept altogether. If we were auctioning or selling clothing that was actually worn by a star on screen, it would have been another story. Then, we would have been saying, for instance, that this was the dress the great Indian cine star Shah Rukh Khan wore in a certain film, and one could possess it

 | If I Had To Do It Again…
Potent Combination for Global Reach

by paying a certain amount. As there would be no second piece, it would be exclusive and would have had a keepsake value.

But here we were proclaiming that we would provide the exact replica of the dresses worn by the stars, and that too custom-made. Our logic was that this would be far more interesting than possessing the original piece, because the original may not have necessarily fitted the buyer. On seeing Aishwarya Rai wear a phenomenal dress on screen, one might just feel that, "all I need is this dress and I would look as beautiful as she does." We were promising that dress. We were promising something very huge.

Offering that kind of a product and service suddenly became very attractive, because everyone, somewhere, carries a hidden desire to look like their star icon. We started identifying a lot of scenes where the stars wore rich Indian ethnic wear. We uploaded those images on the site and offered our customers the exact replicas – custom-made.

Opportunities and Challenges

While we were extremely excited about this new opportunity, there were challenges too. Few of them were:

Copyright issues

Was creating replica of the dresses a copyright violation? We were not sure then, and even after so many years, we are still not sure. Today, we can speak about it because we are not into that business anymore. Back then, we took some chances. We took some liberties.

We had taken an informal legal opinion, where we came to an understanding that the dress designs could be treated similar to dance steps in a movie - meaning if one could copy a certain dance step from a movie at, say, a wedding or a party, then a certain dress made public by a film star could be copied too. We could not clearly specify if it was copyright violation. It was still a grey area, and we took our view of convenience that it should be okay. We had, of course, prepared ourselves to face any objections that would have risen. We also took comfort in the fact that entrepreneurs must take these kinds of risks. Napster might get sued to death, but in the process, did it not create a breakthrough in the industry? We plunged in too. A typical entrepreneurial risk that one had to take, while building a business. We took a calculated one and went ahead with it.

Understanding the Nuances of the Dresses

The second challenge was to learn and understand the design of the dresses worn by the stars in a movie. There was no one showing us the original piece or giving us a view of the dress, or making us understand the type of embroidery used or how exactly it looked from the front or the back. We only had movie scenes to our aid, in which the stars would have worn those clothes. Sometimes, the dress would be part of a song or a dance. We would then try to capture the shot of the dress amid the camera movements. In this manner, with the available information, we would try to visualise the finished product and create the complete dress.

 If I Had To Do It Again…
Potent Combination for Global Reach

However, the interesting bit was that some of our customers spent a lot of time researching on the dresses, perhaps more than what we did. They were so fascinated by the dresses they liked that they wanted to ensure they had the exact replicas and went into great details, sometimes much beyond what we could research. And at times then, they would confront us saying that the dress was not made perfectly – the design did not look the same from the back or that the embroidery was slightly different. It would surprise us as to how they managed to get a view that we had missed. But they would have. In such cases, we would have to negotiate with them. But this was again a part of the risk that we took.

This Challenge was Beyond Us

This challenge was clearly beyond us. People would order a dress worn by a Preity Zinta or a Saif Ali Khan, and would expect to look as attractive as them. In case they did not, even after getting an identical dress from us, they would be disappointed and would somehow find a way to blame us for that. The reality was that they failed to realise that it was not just about the dress in the first place. Now, who would make them understand that there was something called inherent beauty that played a great role in making one look beautiful in whatever one wore.

Anyway, these were some of the challenges. In the larger measure, this line of activity was an absolute success. It gave us an amazing amount of business and visibility, and we became popular.

Our Popularity Grows via Movies

Whenever any movie became popular, we would take the dresses worn by those stars, host them on HomeIndia.com, along with the name of the film and the scenes. Because of this, whenever people looked up for the film or the star, our website began to show up on search engines.

For instance, if people searched for the blue saree that Aishwarya Rai had worn in Devdas, they would see a shot of the film Devdas with her wearing the saree, and also a link to HomeIndia.com, informing them that a replica of the saree could be purchased on the site. The dresses were extremely expensive. Some of them that we had created from the movie Devdas (since Devdas was a classic case, we had made a dress that Madhuri had worn and a saree that Aishwarya had worn) were selling in the range of Rs 75,000 to Rs 1,25,000 each. There were enough customers who were interested and who bought them. These transactions generated high margins for us as well, and Bollywood became a channel for us to generate a great product appeal.

Co-Branding and Association

While we had garnered this visibility on our own, without any partnerships or advertisements, we wondered if we could ally with some business houses and scale up our popularity. Could we formally associate with TV channels or movie banners and become their official merchandise partner? For instance, at the end of every episode of a TV soap opera, could we have a ticker saying - 'Clothing seen in this episode available at HomeIndia.com'? The soap opera would be aired all over the world and we would be tapping into unexplored territories. Similarly, during a movie, could we have had an inset saying – 'You could order some of the clothing shown in the movie at HomeIndia.com'? The reach would then have been phenomenal.

With this in mind, we knocked several doors, hoping to get into some kind of collaboration. We met up with TV channels and approached few film producers, but we were unable to convince them. May be, we were a little ahead of our times or may be, they did not see a large potential in what we were suggesting and felt it was not worth their time. All in all, they were not convinced.

We even thought of getting into deals with, say, film producers, where we would have paid them a certain amount to feature our name in the titles. That would have been a different association altogether. However, on second thoughts, we realised we did not have the kind of money that could be interesting for the film folks.

We did partner in a one-off film - 'Ek Chaalis Ki Last Local.' Unfortunately, the film bombed at the Box Office and the clothing in the movie missed the public eye. We gained very little out of that partnership.

Besides this, there was another association that we got into, which came as a complete surprise, because we had no inkling that such kind of an association would be possible.

A Bollywood dance festival was being organised across 24 German cities - a three-hour Bollywood programme in each city, not with actual Bollywood stars though, but with those who act in Bollywood Theme shows at Broadway. Now, for the surprise element – the cities where the shows were taking place had no significant NRI population. No, these shows were purely catering to an interested German audience!

We realised that Bollywood was quite popular among Germans. Later, after some investigation, we found out that Shah Rukh Khan was quite a heart-throb in Germany, as was Aishwarya Rai in France. Awestruck, we felt the amazing power of Bollywood, especially in Western Europe. Bollywood is believed to be very big in the Middle East and in South East Asia too, but those were not our prime markets.

We got into an association with this German show and managed to get our logo on their posters and brochures. In a barter deal of sorts, we promoted their show on HomeIndia.com. We paid nothing and yet got the visibility among people who were interested in Bollywood, in Germany.

We also tried to associate with bloggers who were writing about Bollywood, and its merchandise. Here again, we found several foreigners blogging about Bollywood, in addition to Indian and NRI bloggers.

There was a particular Swedish blogger, who would analyse every Bollywood film to its minutest detail, including the fashion elements in the films. Her blog was a quite popular, and we associated and interacted with her. She made mentions about HomeIndia.com in some of her blog posts, which gave us decent visibility.

 If I Had To Do It Again…
Potent Combination for Global Reach

Riding on Brands

In short, Bollywood and Indian Television were great vehicles that created a demand for the kind of fashion products that we were offering. As we promoted fashion products based on those TV shows and movies, we managed to garner better visibility and brand popularity for HomeIndia.com. In turn, this contributed significantly to enhance revenues for us, especially at a time when we were struggling to grow our business with negligible marketing budgets. The best bit was that this publicity and this new line of business hardly cost us any serious investment, and yet the benefits we reaped, in terms of profit margins, were very decent.

What we also reckoned was that we could have had viable co-branding or paid-branding opportunities, but at a cost. Since, we did not have the money, we did the next best thing that we could - quietly ride on the shoulder of an existing large brand – Bollywood – and generate visibility for us, but without spending any money.

As a startup or as an entrepreneur, it is interesting to explore the option of third-party brands, whose shoulders you can ride on without having to invest your own money, and still get immeasurable returns. We got one such opportunity and it worked very well for us.

The Wisdom Nugget

> ➤ Risks are an integral part of entrepreneurship. It is just a question of understanding the worst-case scenario when you take the risk. Once that bottom-line is understood and

accepted, and if the risk is still worth taking, then go ahead and take the plunge.

> When budgets are a constraint, there is a larger need for creativity. Especially in the field of marketing. The options then are - to spend money and be a co-branded partner with a successful brand, or to be smart and ride on the shoulders of a successful brand, for free.

If I Had To Do It Again…
Potent Combination for Global Reach

PART III

2005-2007
The Last Mile

The intense struggle after the dotcom bust lasted for four long years. First, it was the struggle to survive, and later to make the company profitable – that too without sufficient marketing budget. Compromises and sacrifices were an integral part of this period. And they took a toll on us – at a personal, professional and family level.

It was a stressful period. But through sheer hard work, we brought our B2C business to profitability. It was a momentous achievement. However, that could hardly be the goal that we were looking for.

It was becoming increasingly clear that we were not fighting this battle just to reach a break-even point, or to just hold our heads above the water. There had to be a bigger game for us.

We had to break away from the hard drag of a survival effort, and make the push for something bigger and better. That is when we embarked on the next phase, which turned out to be "The Last Mile."

Chapter 12

Raising Some More Money

Investors Never Lost Confidence

All the hard work that we had put in during the period 2001-2004 was paying off. By 2005, we were gnawing our way back into a profitable business. Though the profits were very nominal, we were happy that we were not losing money each year, as was the case earlier. We were now able to sustain ourselves without having to worry.

But of course, all this was happening at a huge cost. We had a smaller team – we still could not afford a robust senior management. As founders, we were taking home nominal salaries, just enough to support our families. We still lacked the budget to scale up our business or to do anything substantial. In a nutshell, we lacked serious money and were definitely working under a fair amount of stress. But yes, we had got our business back into black from red. And that was indeed a huge achievement. After all, it had taken four years to make it happen.

Investors Lend Solid Support

As we were re-building our business, our investors strongly rallied behind us. Though it was not like the old times, when investors would jump at any opportunity to invest in dotcom ventures, we still had our occasional conversations with them. In all our interactions, the investors showed confidence in our business model and believed that it was just a matter of time before it became successful. However, being prudent investors who had witnessed the dotcom bust, they did not think it worthwhile to invest more money in our business at that moment. Nor were they in a hurry that we sell off our business so that they could recover their money. In fact, they very well knew the risks involved and were even willing to write off the money, if need be. They gave us guidance especially in those areas where we lacked expertise and encouraged us to tap their connections. They supported us throughout, in the confidence that we would turn the business around. This kept us motivated.

We had survived the dotcom bust and we foresaw that we could be surviving in a similar manner for another four to five years. Perhaps, after that our business would start making a little more than the nominal profit that we were then making. We could have patted ourselves on this achievement, but this was hardly the kind of nominal success that we were looking for. We had got into this business for a certain commercial goal - to generate some serious money for ourselves and our investors. The retail business and the dotcom ventures were big tickets that were meant to make huge money. However, at the rate we were going, the huge money seemed a distant dream and we could also sense that carrying on at the current pace was no wise option either.

 If I Had To Do It Again…
Investors Never Lost Confidence

We decided to do something. We went back to our investors to discuss the proposition of raising the next round of funding. They heard us but were concerned if it was the right thing to do. They wondered if the time was right and whether the market had begun to look at dotcoms favorably yet. After much discussion, they agreed that it might indeed be a good time to raise more money and that we should start talking to people and new investors about the same.

All this was happening while we were directly involved in running the business. We still did not have a team in place to who we could delegate our responsibilities. In short, we could not immediately attend to the raising of funds, but we got back to it in a couple of months.

Raising the Next Round of Funds

To raise the capital, we had to build a robust business plan. This called for a lot of effort. We had survived, but what was the big picture now? What was our growth path? After fair amount of debate and deliberations, we managed to put together a presentation and a spreadsheet describing our plans to achieve the next level of growth and the funds that would be required.

We presented our plan to our investors, and they in turn tapped their connections to check the response in the market. The initial feedback was that the market still did not find our proposal attractive. This brought us to the question – was it worth investing a lot of time pitching to the Venture Capitalists?

As we were pondering over this, our investors who were by now convinced that we should be scaling our business asked us the minimum amount that would be required to give our business at least the first-level push. We reckoned that if the few crores that we desired were going to take some time to materialise, we could settle for a few lakhs – perhaps for a new marketing initiative that would enable us to push our business one notch ahead.

We told them the 'minimum amount' we had in mind. The investors thought about it for some time and finally decided to invest themselves. This was great news because this meant that we need not go through the multiple rounds of meetings and discussions with the new VCs to pitch and to convince them. We could simply work with our existing investors who knew our business thoroughly. They took some time in deciding but once the decision was taken, it was just a matter of them handing us a cheque. With that cheque, we began preparing to give one more level of push to our business.

However, the reality was that the amount was small - much smaller than what we would have liked. We knew that a few lakhs could only give the business a marginal push, but because we got the money without much effort, we became

complacent in our ambition to raise more money. We settled for that small amount and started working with it. We had lost a few precious months in trying to accomplish something big. At the end, the business did move a notch ahead – but only a little.

 | If I Had To Do It Again…
Investors Never Lost Confidence

The bottom line was that it took us several months to raise the money, and then some more time to utilise it. At the end of it, that small amount could only produce small results. We lost a lot of time and yet did not get the big push. All this, of course, is a realisation and the wisdom in the hindsight.

If we look back, when we got the cheque, we were happy to pick up at least that small amount, instead of going out and looking for the larger amount that was really necessary for the business at that time. We felt satisfied that we had an existing group of investors, who were comfortable to write us a cheque and get us going. However, what we should have really done was to challenge ourselves to go out and pitch to new VCs, test our convictions and see if it worked out and whether we were able to raise a larger round then. Even if we had been unable to raise the money, at least we would have tested ourselves. But we did not do that, which was a clear flipside of being in a comfort zone.

The Wisdom Nugget

> ➢ In an entrepreneurial journey, there will be several occasions when you will have a choice of two paths. One will have more challenges but potentially more to gain. A testing path, in a sense. The other path may be an easier pick, less painful, clearly keeping you in the comfort zone. When you are grappling with loads of other challenges, there is always a temptation to pick the easier way. This may be fine at times. But often, that easy choice may be detrimental in the long run.

> Distance yourself from the easy or the difficult part of the choice, but focus only on what it means to the business. If there is a significant benefit in picking the harder choice, go and pick that anyway.

 If I Had To Do It Again…
Investors Never Lost Confidence

Chapter 13

Trade Shows:

Reacting to Changing US Trends, B2B Markets

Non-Indians Become Our Consumers

Significant changes were taking place in the US market. For the first time, we noticed our website attracting non-Indian customers. Where our focus had always been solely on NRIs, we could now see Caucasian Americans and others shopping for Indian clothing on our website. There were several instances when we shipped custom-made wedding gowns for Catholic brides in Western countries. The garment, in fact, was nothing but the traditional Indian choli-sharara repurposed to look like a western bridal gown, embellished with very interesting Indian embroidery. It was a kind of a wedding gown that the bride would not have normally got in a typical satin and lace combination, and that was what set it apart. It was not just the brides who were getting their wedding gowns custom-made from us, but also the bridesmaids and sometimes even the grooms were buying Indian style apparel from us. Besides the expensive designer wear that they were purchasing, they also showed keen interest in our other items like the kurtis and skirts. And what we saw was that this was not an odd exception, but in fact, it was becoming a clear pattern.

At this point, we went and checked out some of the mainline stores in the US like Macy's, J.C Penny and others. Our realisation was proved right. We saw these stores offering a fair amount of Indian style clothing not just to a niche segment, but to the mainstream consumers on top-of-the-line shelves. What this told us was that for certain kind of Indian clothes, there was a mainline acceptance in the Western market. It was not just the Indophiles, but even the regular consumers in those markets showed interest in such Indian products. Seeing this shift in the taste of the American customers, we sensed a very interesting opportunity. Earlier, the challenge was that since our target audience was the NRIs and few Americans who had an India interest, our marketing was extremely fragmented.

We catered to a niche segment and did not have a full-fledged market at any location. But when stores like Macy's began putting up Indian clothes on their display window, we gathered that a reasonable portion of the American mass market was now ready for these Indian products. So, was there a bigger opportunity for us? And if so, how do we grab it?

There was the traditional export channel, through which clothes were sent in bulk from India - what was referred to as the apparel export space. But we were clearly not there. We were not even competing in that space. Those were mass- produced and low-cost exports that probably made it to the show-windows of large stores. What we were offering was stuff with more creativity and by offering them online, we were bypassing the intermediaries. Considering the typical high margins that the big retailers kept for themselves, we reckoned that by bypassing the intermediaries and selling directly, we could deliver our products to the American buyers at a much lower cost. That was the hypothesis. But how do we test this? How do we enter the US market in an effective manner?

Understanding the Concept of Mom-and-Pop Stores

As we investigated whether the large American market was within our reach and how we could seize the opportunity, we identified that there existed a large base of mom-and-pop retail stores in the US. These were small stores, beyond and besides the big box retailers. Operating out of small towns, resort towns, holiday places, and beach hotspots, they were present in large numbers and sold interesting range of popular products. They were often managed by a total of two to three people – usually family members – who did not have the time or the resources to go far to source new, interesting and cost-effective products. In such a case, how did they source their products? Through a prescribed method known as 'trade shows.'

These trade shows happened across several cities in the US, where over three days, a few thousand vendors would put up booths and offer their products. It was largely meant for the small retailers who would come and spend those three days browsing through the various stalls, identifying their products of interest, and finally booking their quantity orders.

When we discovered this particular model, we felt that it was a perfect medium for us to reach the US market. We could go to these trade shows, set up a booth and display some of our products that could be of interest to that market and check if we could get business started for the American retail market.

We researched the US market and identified that it was the West Coast markets that had consumed the maximum number of our Indian products as compared to the rest of the country. This meant that the entire belt from down south California right up to northwest corner in Seattle were the best areas for us to focus on . We refined our research further to figure out the specific categories of our products that could be of interest to an average American. The results showed that ethnic Indian sarees or salwar kameez (our bestsellers, otherwise) would not work. On the other hand, items such as skirts, kurtis, shawls, and accessories like footwear, scarves, interesting ethnic costume jewelry - the kind of items that could be worn with American dresses would fare well in the US market.

Gearing Up to Participate in Tradeshows

As we planned our tradeshow strategy for the US markets, we shortlisted all such product categories and also identified relevant tradeshows along the West Coast.

Interestingly, these shows happened over a period of consecutive days – maybe for the convenience of foreign companies. It was held three days at one place, then there would be a break of two days, and then the next three days in the second city and so on. That way, the exhibitors could choose to participate in multiple shows, moving

 | If I Had To Do It Again…
Reacting to Changing US Trends, B2B Markets

from one show to the next. We realised that was a great way for us to go.

We picked up one show for the first year in Seattle. It was not much of a scientific decision - just that it agreed well with our calendars and our budget, and we had to start somewhere anyway. The costs attached to the show included booking a booth, setting it up, creating the required inventory and shipping them to the US.

We also had to figure out the payment methods because all the while we had been operating via online transactions on the website. But if somebody wanted to purchase our products at the tradeshow and pay us right there, how do we accept the payments? We racked our brains, worked hard and managed to get the offline credit card payment set up.

Then there was the issue of the look and feel of the booth. How do we design a booth in the US? If we were participating in a show of this kind in India, we would have managed to get a fair amount of help in every area. But in the US, we had to manage most of the stuff ourselves. Booth designing and set-up were areas that were unknown to us. However, even this issue had a solution.

We realised that in the US, there were ready solutions for all such requirements. We looked up and found that there were stores that offered on rent everything that one needed to set up a booth. From mannequins to hangers to stands, one just had to figure out what works best, rent out and take them along.

Apart from these, there were other questions playing on our mind. Would we need local help? Would we need somebody to assist us to physically move the products, set up the booth and man it too? We enquired about all these and finally decided to hire some volunteers and interns to help us.

We were slowly getting the pieces of the new puzzle in place.

Final Touches

As far as our inventory was concerned, we developed products as per the categories that we had zeroed down upon and shipped them to a friend's house. Once we reached the US, we collected the boxes and literally moved them in and out of rented cars to the booth. Phew! That involved a fair amount of labour.

Then we went and picked up on rent a few mannequins, a few stands and hangers based on the size of the booth we had. Our brochures were ready and we went about setting up our booth. It was an amazing experience as we slowly

figured out how to set it up and run it too. The whole process of setting up went off quite smoothly.

Our First Tradeshow

The experience at the booth was a new one for us. We had to behave like proper salesmen. As prospects went by the aisles, we had to reach out to them and get them into our booths. We felt like street hawkers, but we did all that unabashedly. It was tiring. Being on your feet all day, talking to people, smiling, making the sales pitch, cracking smart jokes, keeping them in good humour, giving them a

 | If I Had To Do It Again…
Reacting to Changing US Trends, B2B Markets

taste of India – doing all these for three days in succession was not trivial. Add to that, the effort of hauling the large boxes of inventory, setting up the booth every morning and packing it in the evening, dealing with the tradeshow authorities, taking long walks in the show arena to get from one place to the other - all these were quite an effort. It did not matter then that we were the Co-founders and CEOs of the company. During that period, we could have been the loaders, the salesmen, the clerks, the decorators… all rolled into one.

But the best bit was that the tradeshow went off quite well for us. There was a lot of interest in our products and we managed to book a decent amount of orders. We also connected with numerous retailers and this generated a lot of excitement, so much so that where we had planned to do only one trade show in a year, we decided to participate in another one while we were there.

The next one was scheduled for the following weekend at Vancouver, Canada, just an hour's drive from Seattle. That show also turned out to be fairly successful and we walked out with a good number of orders. Boy! Were we excited!

Turning into an Offline Store?

At this juncture, one may find it important to ask us whether we were drifting away into a different kind of a market or a business. Where we were supposed to be building an online store, were we moving towards a traditional export business?

We were looking at the tradeshows as a means to acquire B2B customers. The way we saw it was that the online retail market was growing at a certain pace and the tradeshows were giving us an additional B2B opportunity to sell our products in bulk. Once we had built a rapport at the tradeshow and connected with the retailers, we could induce them to place repeat orders via online rather than physically meeting them each time. This was the business model that we had envisaged - acquire B2B customers and then direct or rather migrate them into a B2B online store for booking repeat orders. That way, we could have a regular B2C and a B2B channel on our website. The experience in both Seattle and Vancouver was very encouraging from this point of view.

These tradeshows happened twice a year – once during the fall and the other during spring. We attended our first show in the fall. After its success, we decided to go for the spring show as well. Meanwhile, we had shipped out our first orders. In few cases, we got repeat orders. Not everyone placed repeat orders, but again, we felt that it would need a certain buildup time. We also felt that we should go and meet the clients once more to establish a proper B2B sales channel. With that thought, we were soon ready to go again.

Gearing for the Second Show

The money we had raised initially was invested in our first tradeshow. While both the shows made us well-known in the tradeshow circle and enabled us to garner decent business, the money that we had raised was completely spent. The orders that we had picked up gave us only nominal margins and it was not enough to cover the cost of taking part in the trade show the second time. We had no option but to go back to our investors. We briefed them about our success

 | If I Had To Do It Again…
Reacting to Changing US Trends, B2B Markets

and asked them to invest some more money so that we could do one more show before we established the business model. They readily agreed.

While preparing for the second show, we took some learning from the previous show. Both of us had attended the first show and we had found that one of the key requirements was to instantly address the orders that we had picked up, and to ship out the products at the earliest. To make this possible in the second show, we decided that only one of us would go and the other would stay back to coordinate the shipments. That decided, we set to work on our inventory. This time, we got a little more ambitious and carried with us more variety of products. We also decided to do three cities instead of two – Los Angeles, San Francisco and Seattle. LA and San Francisco were definitely bigger markets compared to Seattle. We were very confident that our second show would be far better than the first.

Second Show Unlike the First One

We participated in the show. The booth was set up, the brochures in place. Everything was the same except that the whole market in spring was very different from the market during fall. It was a different season and attracted a different nature of products – completely different from the fall. Our products somehow did not generate the desired traction in this season and failed to get too many takers!

With all the hard work that we had put in, the additional inventory that we had carried, the additional number of cities that we chose to attend (more expensive ones too), with all the extra preparations that we put in - this second adventure actually did not fare well at all. Our performance was far poorer than the first one. It was indeed a great disappointment. As the response was pale, we could not sell much of our inventory and were left with a lot of unsold products. We decided to leave the excess inventory at a friend's place in the US, with the idea that once we put them up for sale on our website, she could quickly ship them as and when we got the orders.

While we were attending the shows, we also investigated the rest of the trade ecosystem in the US for our kind of products. What we found was that apart from these shows that took place twice a year in different cities, there were also full-fledged buildings that had small outlets of product companies. A mom-and-pop business could come to any of these outlets at any time of the year and find products that they may want to buy. Not that we wanted to take up a place in one of those buildings, but we figured that we could work with some of the people who already had an establishment in these buildings because they were reaching out to the same market that we desired to through the shows. We did the rounds of a large number of such buildings, established relations with some of them and even managed to get some orders.

Realisation

All in all, between the tradeshows and the permanent small stores in the market place buildings, we managed to get a certain amount of business, but much less than what we had expected.

 | If I Had To Do It Again…
Reacting to Changing US Trends, B2B Markets

This experience led us to realise that this whole business with the retailers was based on relationships. The retailers would want to see us every year because that was how we would be forging a bond with them. We realised that for a B2B market, it was not about knowing a name or a website; it was more about developing a one-on-one understanding with buyers. We also realised that we had to be prepared to build relationships for several years, attend tradeshows regularly, meet and build connections with them till they became our regular customers.

This also meant that we had to be present in the US more regularly to meet the retailers, which was clearly a departure from our original business model. And of course there would be a huge cost involved every time we would visit the US. If we had budgeted our expenses in a manner that we would be attending tradeshows for five years or so, it would have made sense. But the whole idea that we would initially sell the retailers the products at one or two tradeshows and that they would then place repeat orders via our online store did not seem to be happening – the conversion of customer base from offline to online definitely seemed to be a far cry.

Another understanding that we got from the two rounds was that the two seasons were quite different from each other! Due to seasonal preferences, the same kind of products may not work well in both the seasons. Again this learning came after a lot of research and the actual trials that happened in terms of our participation. Bottom line was that there was no short cut to entering a new market!

All in all, there was a lot of learning from this whole tradeshow exercise. It was a huge experiment – to be there, to put up the booth, and to sell our products at a trade show. But after two tradeshows, we concluded that the model we were pursuing was not right for us. We had invested a lot of money but it did not pay back. That spelt the end of the experiment. Considering the expenses we had incurred, we kind of booked a financial loss. We took this as a part of our entrepreneurial journey. This experiment was something that we had to undertake to capture a bigger market in a short time. It was a calculated risk – in this case, it did not quite work out for us. However if it had worked out, we would have been on a different and very interesting path.

You sometimes have to go by the gut. Some things may work out, some things may not. It is like - nothing ventured, nothing gained. We ventured and we learnt a lot. We can safely say that we had no regrets about this experiment, but yes, it was one that did not quite work out.

The Wisdom Nugget

➤ Generating scale is the only way to make a venture truly successful. And that may often require you to take some bold calls. An entrepreneur has to take those calls from time to time. And not all of those calls may work out.

➤ But like mentioned before - nothing ventured, nothing gained. And that's how the entrepreneurship route goes.

Chapter 14

Jewelry E-Retail, Youth Markets

It was a Changed Landscape

With the tradeshows not turning out to be a good option for us, we were again at the crossroads, trying to figure out 'what next' for our business? Looking back, we had done our survival bit, pulled the business out of many challenges and made it profitable. But we still needed a bigger picture.

By now, we were in the middle of 2005-06. The market was looking up and investment channels were once again beginning to view dotcoms favourably. Having seen a few dotcom companies survive and do good business after the dotcom bust in 2000-01, the investors were willing to have a relook at them. This gave us hope. We figured that this was a good time to talk to the Venture Capitalists again and narrate to them our survival story – of how we had toiled hard to pull our business back to profit and how it was now poised for significant growth, provided we had the required capital.

With that in mind, we began talking to a couple of investors whom we knew. After few such meetings, we came to a shocking realisation. While the investors had returned to reconsider dotcom investment opportunities in India, the one thing that had significantly changed this time was their market focus. What was interesting them now was the emerging Indian consumer space.

Emergence of the Indian Consumer Market

The Indian market, by this time, had grown a lot stronger with a good section of the working force having a decent disposable income. This attracted investors towards businesses that could actually thrive on this large market opportunity. Apart from India, China was equally an attractive market. But our focus was neither India nor China. All the while, our target audience had been Indians outside India – mainly in the US. We were clearly not selling anything to anyone in India. However, the investors who were earlier not considering India were now looking at Indian consumers, as this was the market that was expanding and any business that could thrive on the bulging Indian market would be attractive to them.

Having understood this, we were again in a dilemma. On one side, we had learnt the ropes of e-commerce and e-retail business the hard way and probably knew a lot more about it than most people in India. On the other side, e-commerce and dotcoms were back, but the marketplace was different. We had a global market exposure, but the investors now preferred the domestic market. Would it be wise then to still go back to the investors and convince them about our global market prowess? The truth was that the investors showed less interest in our proposition and the market that we were addressing - a dispersed NRI and a niche global market that was not quite so dynamic and exciting. In such a case, should we continue to fight

 | If I Had To Do It Again…
It was a Changed Landscape

hard for our business or should we consider flipping our business model to cater to the Indian consumers?

From the market point of view, the latter would have been a fresh start because we had not yet sold to Indians in India. Yes, catering to this consumer segment would have come with its own set of challenges, but at least we knew the fundamentals of online selling quite well. We began considering how to flip our business model and focus on the market opportunity in the Indian consumer space. However, we were yet to ascertain whether we could keep everything else the same and just start offering the products to the Indian market, whether the categories or the products that we were selling could be equally interesting and attractive for India, or whether changes were necessary on those fronts.

Shifting Focus to a New Target Audience

Our big ticket category had been fashion and apparel – women's apparel, embroidered products, sarees, and the like. When we thought about this category from an Indian market perspective, we were unsure. Weren't there enough apparel stores at every street corner, where people could walk in and try out the clothing to their entire satisfaction before purchasing them? The apparel category was popular in the foreign market because such stores were few and far between there, but for India, would this be an attractive market? We had severe doubts about it.

The whole exercise suddenly began to seem unworthy. First, we were trying to flip our business model to cater to the Indian audience and then we were zeroing down on a product category that we ourselves had doubts about. Things did not look very positive to us.

We sat back to discuss - if not apparel, then what? If not sarees, clothing and jewellery, then what else could we sell to the Indians in India? This sounded like desperate thinking, where just because we wanted to sell something, we were

figuring out what could be sold. This is not exactly how a business plan should be built. But we were at our wit's ends, having spent so much time and having done so much in the e-commerce space that we were trying desperately to find something interesting to sell to the Indian consumers on an e-retail basis.

It was a challenge indeed to figure out a good business opportunity. And we repeat - this is not how a business plan should be built. But left with no choice, we worked hard to see if we could find an opportunity. A couple of interesting ideas did emerge. We will ponder over these ideas only to emphasize the fact that the learning we had gathered over the past five to six years enabled us to come up with some interesting opportunities.

For example, we had learned from the NRI market that a genuine product need, which is not easily met, could be a very interesting business opportunity. So, were there product categories in India that could be a need but were not easily available? We wondered. Similarly, another understanding from our previous global exposure was that there was a premium on custom-fitting, and that it was a clear need for many people. The learning was that if there was a service element to your product offering - something that was

 | If I Had To Do It Again...
It was a Changed Landscape

not easily available to the people, then maybe that was an edge you could build on.

Taking cue from these learning, we actually came up with two options of product categories. Both drew inspiration from the fact that the youth would comprise a large section of the current and future Internet user base in India. Internet then was largely adopted by the youth and even today continues to be so. In such a case, it was but natural that our product categories should be targeted to appeal to the youth.

Merchandise for the Youth

Having spent a lot of time in the US as students and later for business purposes, we had seen that the West had an extremely large market of product offerings for the youth. India had not yet reached that level. We sensed this as a business opportunity.

For example, within the Universities in the West, there were very large stores catering only to the college students, providing them literally everything that they would need. It was an aggregation of a number of products that the students would need, offered under one roof. This was indeed a huge business, where each store probably did at least a few million dollars of business. Such stores were located typically outside all US Universities and at various schools and colleges as well.

Considering the fact that Indians regarded education to be extremely important and that we had an overall sizeable population, India consequentially also had one of the largest student populations, with small, mid-sized and large-sized colleges catering to them. We reckoned that these were our prime candidates who could be offered a large range of relevant products. We began visualising a store for that market base. We built the business plan, created product categories, worked out excel sheets for business modeling, costs, supply sources, margins, chalked out how products would get delivered, et al. We planned out everything. That became our new business plan and we were pretty excited about it. To add an element of expansion, we decided to also offer, what is referred to as college merchandising. This was actually our original and bigger idea.

Again, we took our learning from the West. In the West, there were three very large merchandising markets – the first one based on sports, where the merchandiser includes sports teams' based T-shirts, caps, jerseys, jackets, shoes and such other items. Sports was one big merchandising category - encompassing all types of sports like football, baseball, basketball, tennis, golf and so on.

The second merchandising opportunity was in entertainment – Hollywood, Music and other such segments. They would have a whole range of product offerings like posters, T-shirts, say, around popular Hollywood movies, superhero characters, film stars, music bands, music albums, etc.

The third category was college merchandise, where they would develop merchandise for every college – say a whole range of T-shirts, caps and several other such items. The students who were already in the college as well as the alumni would consume the merchandise with a sense of pride.

We tried to match these opportunities with the Indian market. We realised that sports in India was largely about cricket and cricket merchandising was happening to a certain extent. Again, it was a relatively controlled market with the Board of Control for Cricket in India wanting to have their say in everything related to cricket. In terms of entertainment, some Indian films had tried to create merchandise around their films. As far as music was concerned, it was not that popular in terms of merchandise. Which left us with the third category - the school/college merchandising!

In this category, we saw an untapped opportunity. We wondered why and how it had remained untapped for so long. Maybe, as a developing country, the disposable income must have been low for students to afford additional college-branded T-shirts and other such accessories. But now the situation was changing - with an emerging middle class and a larger disposable income, it was perhaps the right time to venture into college merchandising. What if we could create the largest college merchandise store in India, to an extent that we give the students the flexibility to even personalise their products? A youth merchandise store, with an extension of college merchandising, college branding, and personalization of products seemed like a phenomenal idea in terms of the volume opportunity.

We again sat down to put together a whole new business plan, after which we began meeting the VCs. While there was a lot of excitement after we met a couple of investors, we could not immediately strike a deal. Each time we met a new investor and went through the whole process of presenting our case and trying to convince them, we could feel our energy draining away. We thought we had good ideas, but every time the investors would confront us with questions like – without any experience in the Indian market, how did you expect to flip your business model? What happens to the business you had already created? These were questions to which even we did not have any convincing answers. Frustration was slowly seeping in. After all, we had spent a good six to seven years in this business and had put in a lot of struggle. Somewhere, we were getting tired and our mental framework at that moment was definitely not at its best.

A New Opportunity and a Host of Realisations

Meanwhile, there was another development. An exporter from a large jewellery firm called on us. He exported jewellery in bulk to global customers and had a business to the tune of about Rs 2000 crore. He was an ace at jewellery and diamond business but had no clue about the online space. This was why he had reached out to us. Over time, we had built a good personal network and a lot of people in the marketplace knew us as pioneers in the Internet space. They recognised us for our solid e-commerce knowledge and understanding. He felt he could use our knowledge in setting up a branded online jewellery store in India. He felt the time had come when India could have such a store. He wanted us to abandon our website, HomeIndia.com, and join forces with him to build and lead the jewellery e-retail portal. We had a long chat with him, checked out his factory, understood his product range, and discussed the opportunity at length.

 If I Had To Do It Again…
It was a Changed Landscape

We were tempted to take the offer as those were desperate times. Having spent so much time in the industry, we were wondering whether we could make something out of our experience. If we were unable to flip our business model to cater to the Indian audience, could we at least use our expertise to begin afresh? None of these thoughts would have emerged if our original venture had taken off in the right path and we had generated enough money to scale up our business. But the reality was that even after six to seven years of hard work, we were desperate to find ways and means to give some meaning to the time we spent in the e-commerce space, to create something useful out of our experience. It was disheartening, yet we explored new ideas with an open mind.

The fact is that, as an entrepreneur, you may notice a changing landscape. Instead of moving away from what you had originally set out to do, you could look at salvaging your experience and making something out of it. From that point of view, we considered pursuing this new opportunity.

However, we ultimately figured out that we did not want to take up the new opportunity. We also figured out that if it was not going to be HomeIndia.com, we might as well wind up and make something else out of our lives, rather than trying to flog the horse some more. We realised that we were trying to somehow cling on to a path that we had earlier chosen. Options were available – be it Indian retail or diamond retail.

But the reality was that we had to make a fresh start. In such a case, we must first disengage from HomeIndia.com and then look at opportunities afresh - be it youth merchandise or diamond e-retail.

For that matter, then why limit ourselves to just these two options? We felt we must clean our current slate and then think hard on what to do next, rather than simply picking up whatever it was that came along.

Those were hard times. Those were tough times, as we slowly started to accept a tough reality.

The Wisdom Nugget

> ➤ An entrepreneur's sprit refuses to relent even in the face of deep adversity. Over a period of 10 years, we had evolved the business from Internet seminars to web-sites development to Online Post to Online Gifting to Online Shopping to offering customised fashion-wear to being a B2B supplier to trade. While we were achieving limited success, we were unable to generate the kind of volumes required to convert it into a big profitable business. But still, the entrepreneurial spirit continued to explore avenues after avenues.

 If I Had To Do It Again…
It was a Changed Landscape

Chapter 15

Putting the Company on the Block:

Mixed Emotions

We had limited options and somewhere clarity was slowly dawning on the next steps to be taken.

Weighing Our Options

One option was to continue the way we were – growing at a small scale. With the limited amount of money that we had, this was probably the only option if we had to continue the business. We had realised that our current business model was incapable of attracting the large infusion of capital required for a significant growth. The investors were reluctant to invest in our NRI-focused business, as their interest was into pure Indian-market-focussed businesses. In such a scenario, if we had to continue, we had no choice but to continue to grow at the small scale that we could afford. But did we actually want that?

The second option was to shift our consumer base to Indians in India. That would mean a fresh start, but we somewhere felt that it was not the right thing to do at that point of time.

Then there were other options - like getting into a completely new business, say, jewellery e-retail or something similar. That would again have been a fresh start because these businesses would have been in no way related to HomeIndia.com. We felt that this was again not an apt option for HomeIndia.com. Rather, if at all, it was an option AFTER HomeIndia.com.

Recognising these harsh realities and weighing each option, where none looked any better than the other, we had to take some very tough calls. Those were extremely difficult times - as we had been in the business for a good eight to nine years. Somewhere, the business had become us and we had become the business. In Hindi, you could say that the business had become our 'astitva' – our identity. We were recognised for HomeIndia.com and HomeIndia.com for us. To consider a life beyond our business seemed extremely challenging. It was our baby, who we had given birth to and nurtured for all these years. We had fond memories - of having bootstrapped a business from scratch, having seen a whole bunch of ups and of course, a whole lot of downs. Was it actually a business that we had to exit from? Emotions were running very high.

Accepting the Reality and Taking the Tough Calls

That was one side of the story. The other was that we clearly understood that we had put in prime years of our career into this business. Where we could have been in comfortable jobs or managing our family businesses, we chose to do something of our own. But the reality was that, in doing this, and since the desired result had

 If I Had To Do It Again…
Mixed Emotions

not happened ultimately, we had missed out on key productive years for creating wealth for ourselves and our families. We had earned enough to keep our family going but when we looked at the life that lay ahead of us, we reckoned that we had not built much capital – money that could take care of our future. We also realised that the more we lingered and the more we hung around, we were losing more of our crucial years and not creating the desired wealth during this period. We recognised and understood these stark realities but the problem was that we were yet to accept them. Our passion for HomeIndia.com was allowing a lot of doubts to crop up in our minds. This, in turn, was delaying us from taking tough decisions. Very unlike a corporate career, where one could have simply moved out and taken a new job elsewhere.

After so many years of "being" HomeIndia.com, among the doubts we had, the most pertinent one was - what would we do next if we exited HomeIndia.com? While we had absolutely no doubts about our personal capabilities and the learning we had had through HomeIndia.com, we still wondered what we could be doing at the age of 43 or 44, if we weren't working for HomeIndia.com. Who would employ us? We did not have a rich corporate experience to showcase. Sometimes, it is these types of insecurities about the future that forces one to cling onto the present, even when the present is not the best situation one could be in.

On second thoughts, both of us had actually been very successful in our academic careers and in whatever else we did, including this venture. The way we had built HomeIndia.com, irrespective of the fact that the end result had not turned out to be as profitable as we would have liked, was commendable indeed. We knew that we had created something special and seriously believed we were meant for bigger and better things.

With the fear of 'what next' aside and recognising that HomeIndia. com was not leading us anywhere substantial, we finally bit the bullet and took that tough call. We decided to get out of it. We felt we had already over-stayed and it was now or never. We had clearly given it more than 110 percent, but maybe the timing was not quite right. Or perhaps, we were ahead of our times. Whatever be the case, we realised that we had to move on and do something else in life.

How Best to Exit?

That decision taken, the next question was – how do we exit? What was the best we could do? Could we just wind up, sell off all our assets, liquidate everything and walk away? Or was there a better way out?

We recognised that we had built an interesting asset in HomeIndia. com. The fact that we were located at a small office in Lower Parel and that we were able to sell bridal wear online to some lady getting married in Michigan in the US was by no means a small feat. Not only that, but that the brides were willing to spend thousands of dollars on our website day after day proved that we had created something of value. How much was that value and who was going to pay us that amount was something that we did not know. But we felt that there was indeed a great value for what we had built.

 If I Had To Do It Again…
Mixed Emotions

Putting HomeIndia.com on the Block

With that in mind, our initial efforts were directed towards finding out if we could sell our venture. Unlike the earlier days when HomeIndia.com had attracted large valuations, it was going to be difficult now as times had changed.

We wanted to salvage whatever we could. Hence, we decided to package it well, create a document about what the business was all about and look around for buyers. We formally put the business on the block.

Usually, such businesses are sold through merchant bankers who take the mandate to find the right buyers. But that is when the markets are bullish, and there are a lot of buyers looking for good deals and for assets that are appreciating.

However, the situation where we were in, much as we would have liked to camouflage it, appeared like a bit of a distress situation. This was not exactly the impression that the market should have of you, especially when you are trying to sell something.

Nevertheless, we spoke to a few merchant bankers to take up the sale of our business, but they were not very keen. Maybe, the success fee also had a role to play. They got paid a percentage of the transaction once the deal was completed. In our case, the transaction value would not have been too large. Moreover, they would not have been able to find buyers easily, as our business was not a hot property. Hence, they did not seem too keen to take up the mandate for the sale of our venture. It was very disheartening. How do we now let the word out that we were up for sale? It was not easy for us to tap the buyers individually and let them know we were selling our venture. This was where we decided to explore other opportunities.

Why not tap businesses similar to ours in the same domain and look at a possible opportunity to join hands with them? Maybe, together we could make it bigger. This sounded like an idea worth pursuing.

By now, there were several companies like us, who were selling ethnic Indian products to customers outside India. Among them, there was one company whom we knew reasonably well - ChennaiBazaar.com, which also had a brand name called CBazaar. com. We chose to open up a conversation with them. They were based out of Chennai and, like us, were promoted by two friends. Probably, they had started a couple of years after us and might have been a little smaller than us, in terms of revenue. The fact was that they were self funded, and due to lack of larger marketing capital, even they were struggling to grow rapidly. More or less, we both were in a similar boat.

Since we knew each other, the four of us decided to meet up and explore the idea. We had our operations in Mumbai and they had it in Chennai, and we both had the same target audience. In such a case, why not combine the operations to one and service the market together? Wouldn't this ensure better efficiency, thereby making the whole business more viable such that it starts generating better profits? This was the initial idea which was discussed at length.

As a concept, it made a lot of sense and appeared quite feasible. While everything sounded perfect, we began wondering the role the four of us would play. After all, even after the merger, the business was not going to become very large, just yet. Then, would the business need all the four of us to be actively involved? This thought led the discussions to a different direction – what if we combine the two businesses but consolidate these at one end? This meant that one of us would buy the other out. Somewhere, we were slowly going back to where we began - our search for someone who could buy our venture.

In case we chose to be bought out, then the scenario would have been that HomeIndia.com would still continue to run and we would get some value for giving up our stake. This seemed like an interesting option, especially when it seemed tough to find any buyers to acquire our venture. We decided to pursue the option. However, as mentioned before, ChennaiBazaar.com was like us, a small sized company and did not have a large capital to acquire us for cash. Hence, our original expectation to sell the company and get a decent return seemed unlikely to happen. Rather, a different option emerged.

∞

ChennaiBazaar.com would buy our inventory so that we did not have to liquidate any stock, and we, in turn, would get a stake in their company (the consolidated venture.) We would wind up the operations in Mumbai but the brand would continue, and be transferred to them. We would exit out of

HomeIndia.com operations, would not manage anything and would not have any active role to play. We would simply be financial investors in their venture.

Left with not much choice, this seemed like a reasonable option. After all, our hard work was at least giving us something back – even if it was in terms of equity and not cash.

Curtains Down

We discussed the deal as much as possible and finally took one of the hardest calls of our lives – to bid farewell to our precious business that we had so passionately built.

We soon finalised the format and went ahead to create the joint entity. Finally, CBazaar or ChennaiBazaar.com – promoted by Rajesh Nahar and Ritesh Katariya, and HomeIndia.com – promoted by Sanjay Mehta and Hareesh Tibrewala, consolidated. We held a tiny hope that maybe our equity in the new Joint Venture may lead to something worthwhile in the future. Meanwhile, for now we could go out and make a fresh start of our lives!

It was not as profitable an exit as we would have liked, but it was an honourable one. Hard bullets have to be bitten sometimes and this was one such bullet that we had to bite. It was a tough call but we went ahead with it because what had to be done, had to be done. This was how our HomeIndia.com story came to end for us.

 If I Had To Do It Again…
Mixed Emotions

The Wisdom Nugget

- ➤ You've tried everything.

- ➤ You worked hard. Very hard.

- ➤ You sacrificed. You gave it time. Perhaps more than adequate time. You pivoted. And then pivoted some more.

- ➤ In short, you did all that you could.

- ➤ But still things did not work out.

- ➤ If fate lands you in a situation of this kind and you find yourself at wit's end, then and only then think of how you can make a decent exit. This would be in the interest of your future.

- ➤ Everyone works for a glorious and successful finish. But should that not happen, don't just dump the venture. An honorable, dignified exit is in the interest of all stakeholders and it will keep your goodwill alive.

Epilogue

An entrepreneur can be easily compared to a soldier. When a soldier fights for his country, he does not quite care if he will win a medal or come back in a body bag. Doing his duty is all that he cares for. Similarly, for an entrepreneur, his mission to accomplish a successful business is all that he cares for. And in case the business fails to succeed, the people who usually take the brunt are his family members.

At a personal level, our decade long journey at establishing HomeIndia.com as a pioneer Internet venture was thoroughly fulfilling and satisfying, even if it did not manage to reach a financially desirable conclusion. Hence, post HomeIndia.com, it was time to take care of our families.

Both of us took up jobs in the corporate world and worked as professionals for two years. This probably helped take care of our families' financial needs. However, an entrepreneur's spirit simply refuses to die and so the joy of a driving around in a chauffeur-driven-sedan or zigzagging across the globe or seeing a guaranteed paycheck credited to the bank account every month was short-lived for us. We wanted to be entrepreneurs once again. After all, as an entrepreneur, even if your kingdom is small, you are still the king.

Hence, while we were still in our respective jobs, we met up one evening for dinner. Some seeds for a new entrepreneurial opportunity started germinating in our heads. Over the next few months, a business plan got firmed up. Subsequently, both of us quit our respective jobs and launched a new venture called 'Social Wavelength' in 2009.

We made excellent use of all our learning from HomeIndia.com and it was just a matter of few years that Social Wavelength became India's largest social media agency. Later in 2014, it was acquired by a large global advertising agency.

Both of us continue to manage this business actively till date (along with a third partner, Mihir Karkare), and hope to do so for a long time to come.

Media writes only about successful entrepreneurs. But we need to realise that for every one Mark Zuckerberg or Bill Gates or Dhirubhai Ambani, there are probably a few hundred entrepreneurs who are finding it difficult to bring food to the table for their families. Our book is a tribute to all those entrepreneurs who may not get written about in the press or make it to a large fortune…but who nevertheless have contributed and are still contributing to the religion of entrepreneurship.

Dear Reader

The price of a book is not the amount of money you pay for buying the book. But the amount of your precious time that you have invested in reading it. And for that we thank you. The name of the book goes – ***If I Had To Do It Again***, and we are proud to say that '*we did it again*,' with Social Wavelength. And in time, it will be a pleasure to narrate the experiences attached to this new venture in our next book!

Au Revoir till then,

Sanjay Mehta   **Hareesh Tibrewala**
June 2015

www.ingramcontent.com/pod-product-compliance
Lightning Source LLC
Chambersburg PA
CBHW020757150726
48196CB00001B/64